About This Issue

We are pleased to publish this collection of articles by colleagues and former students in honor of the distinguished historian, Jay P. Dolan. His books and articles on the social and religious history of American Catholicism have been widely acclaimed; his stature as a leading figure in promoting new areas of research in several spheres of the American Catholic experience will long be remembered by a generation of historians. These achievements have been recognized by his peers in the profession, symbolized by his election to the presidency of the American Society of Church History and to the American Catholic Historical Association. Only John Tracy Ellis, Martin E. Marty, and Albert C. Outler have been presidents of both professional societies. As founder and long-time director of the Cushwa Center for the Study of American Catholicism, Jay Dolan has brought together hundreds of scholars who have experienced stimulating conferences and seminars in an atmosphere of genuine conviviality. On behalf of a generation of historians, thank you Jay Dolan and happy retirement!

We are grateful to the contributors to this special issue. R. Scott Appleby is the Director of the Joan B. Kroc Institute for International Peace Studies at the University of Notre Dame. We welcome Scott as a consulting editor of our journal. Jeffrey M. Burns, who graciously organized this tribute to his mentor, is archivist of the Archdiocese of San Francisco. Kathleen Sprows Cummings is a Lilly Fellow at Valparaiso University in Valparaiso, Indiana. Philip Gleason is Professor Emeritus of History at the University of Notre Dame. Mary Linehan is Associate Professor of History at Spalding University in Louisville, Kentucky. Martin E. Marty is the Fairfax M. Cone Distinguished Service Professor Emeritus of the History of Modern Christianity at the University of Chicago, and is presently a member of the advisory board of the Marty Center for Research in Public Religion in the Divinity School. Anita Specht is Assistant Professor of History at Kansas Wesleyan University in Salina, Kansas. Joseph M. White, an independent historian, has recently completed the history of the Franciscans of the Holy Name Province.

—CJK

About This Journal

It is a pleasant coincidence that this special issue in honor of Jay P. Dolan is the first number of the U.S.C.H. published by the University of Notre Dame Press. As an academic journal we are indeed fortunate to be associated with a university press that has such a fine tradition of quality publications. We look forward to working with Barbara Hanrahan, Director, Jeffrey Gainey, Associate Director, and Wendy McMillen, Production Manager.

—CJK

A Half-Century of Change
in Catholic Higher Education

Philip Gleason

O ver the past half-century, the development of Catholic colleges and universities in the United States has been shaped by two upheavals of earthquake proportions—World War II and "the Sixties." By "the Sixties," I mean to designate, not just the religious changes set off by the Second Vatican Council, but also the broader national crisis that gripped American society in that decade, particularly after 1965. The effects of the Sixties, thus understood, are more dramatic than those associated with World War II, but we begin with the latter because they came first and profoundly influenced the subsequent development of American higher education.

World War II and American Higher Education

The impact of World War II was most clearly marked in the tremendous boost it gave to college enrollments. The Servicemen's Readjustment Act of 1944 provided federal funding to cover tuition, incidental educational costs, and living expenses of veterans who wished to go to college. Upwards of 8 million former servicemen and women took advantage of these provisions of the "G.I. Bill of Rights," as it was popularly known.[1] That tidal wave of students almost overwhelmed the nation's colleges and universities, but the G.I. Bill also had a more lasting effect—it drove home and democratized the understanding that higher education opened the way to upward social mobility. In the era of sustained postwar prosperity, a vast new segment of the American population came to look upon college as the normal follow-up to high school. This in turn created an imperative demand for college teachers; as a result, graduate education entered upon an era of unprecedented growth and faculties mushroomed. Even before the baby-boom generation set off another burst of expansion in the 1960s,

---

1. See Keith W. Olson, *The G.I. Bill, the Veterans and the Colleges* (Lexington, Ky., 1974).

higher education had become a leading growth sector of the "knowledge industry" and a major new site for gainful employment of the choicest white-collar variety.[2]

No segment of the population benefitted more spectacularly from these trends than American Catholics. In 1955, a respected sociologist concluded on the basis of data published in the late forties that the social status of his fellow Catholics was not much higher than it had been in the middle of the previous century. Twelve years later, the authors of an article reviewing eighteen national surveys taken between 1943 and 1965 reported strikingly different findings: Catholics had, during that span of years, moved up so rapidly that they stood higher than Protestants (but not Jews) on most measures of social status. Catholics were at last "making it"—leaving the immigrant era behind and being assimilated as full-fledged Americans. But assimilation affected the mental outlook of American Catholics, as well as their income levels and residential patterns. In time, that would make it more difficult to maintain a distinctive Catholic intellectual stance, or even to see why one should try to do so.[3]

In the meantime, Catholic institutions of higher education were carried along in the postwar boom. Between 1945 and 1965, they increased in number by one-third, from 169 to 224 four-year institutions for lay students; in the same period, enrollments grew from about 232,000 to 402,000 (a 73% increase), while the number of faculty members more than doubled (from 13,636 to 30,279).[4] There was comparable expansion at the graduate level. Doctoral level work had hardly begun anywhere except at the Catholic University of America when the war broke out: only 103 doctorates were conferred by Catholic institutions in 1940, almost half of them by CUA. In the decade 1955–1964, however, fifteen Catholic institutions produced upwards of 3,300 doctorates. Impressive growth, to be sure, but still a minuscule share (3.1%) of the 104,139 doctorates awarded by American universities in those years.[5]

---

2. See Richard M. Freeland, *Academia's Golden Age: Universities in Massachusetts, 1945–1970* (New York, 1992), esp. chap. 2.

3. John J. Kane, "The Social Structure of American Catholics," *American Catholic Sociological Review*, 16 (March 1955): 23–30; Norval D. Glenn and Ruth Hyland, "Religious Preference and Worldly Success: Some Evidence from National Surveys," *American Sociological Review*, 32 (February 1967): 73–85. For discussion of Catholic assimilation, see Philip Gleason, *Keeping the Faith: American Catholicism Past and Present* (Notre Dame, Ind., 1987), chap. 3.

4. Derived from *Summary of Catholic Education, 1945–1946* (NCWC, 1948) and *Summary of Catholic Education, 1964 and 1965* (USCC, 1967). The statistics for enrollment and faculty include 29 junior colleges in 1945/6 and 26 junior colleges in 1965. Unless otherwise noted, the statistics that follow are all derived from the NCWC/USCC biennial surveys of Catholic education. For specialized studies based on statistics gathered in 1947–48 and 1965–66, respectively, see James F. Whelan, S.J., *Catholic Colleges in the United States of America at the Middle of the Twentieth Century* ([mimeo] New Orleans, 1952); and Charles E. Ford and Edgar L. Roy, Jr., *The Renewal of Catholic Higher Education* (Washington, 1968). Considerable variation exists in statistical reports on Catholic higher education because of differences in how institutions and students are classified.

5. Philip Gleason, "American Catholic Higher Education: A Historical Perspective," in Robert Hassenger, ed., *The Shape of Catholic Higher Education* (Chicago, 1967), 42–43.

Rapid growth of the lay faculty in Catholic institutions accompanied the general expansion. For though religious vocations burgeoned after the war, they could not keep pace with the demand for college professors, especially as more schools undertook graduate work, which was understood to be the hallmark of a "real university." By 1965, lay men and women accounted for four out of five faculty members in the 90 four-year institutions for men included in the biennial survey of Catholic education carried out by the National Catholic Welfare Conference. Although that report does not differentiate between colleges and universities, we can safely assume the lay proportion was considerably higher in the latter, since lay people accounted for almost three-fourths of the faculties of Catholic institutions classified as "universities" on the eve of World War II. The younger segment of the growing lay faculties were among the most assimilated of American Catholics.

Catholic colleges for women kept pace with the general expansion in terms of numbers of schools, but religious continued to dominate their faculties to a greater degree than in men's schools or coeducational institutions. As compared to the 4–to–1 lay/clerical ratio in universities and men's colleges, Catholic women's colleges in 1965 were still predominantly staffed by religious.[6] A special feature of the situation among women religious was the Sister Formation Movement. An indirect outgrowth of the postwar need for teachers, the Sister Formation Conference, which was formally organized in 1954, aimed at combining better professional training with the spiritual formation of sister-teachers. To carry out these aims, nearly a hundred small specialized schools known as "juniorates," "motherhouse colleges," or "Sister-Formation colleges," had come into being by 1960; many were short-lived, but others later transformed themselves into conventional colleges for lay students. Besides adding to the number of Catholic schools, the Sister Formation Movement introduced a complicating element into the authority structure of religious communities of women and reflected a new stage in the assimilation of Catholic women religious to the educational and cultural norms of American society.[7]

In addition to sparking a massive surge in college enrollments, World War II marked the opening of a new era in terms of intensive interaction between the federal government and institutions of higher education. Aside from a short-lived military training program on college campuses in 1918, the federal government had virtually nothing to do with higher education until the second World War. Then a number of military programs provided a much-needed supply of male students for hundreds of colleges,

---

6. According to the NCWC survey for 1965, sisters constituted 52% of the faculties of these schools. A 1959–60 survey of 93 Catholic women's colleges found 63% of the teaching staff were sisters. See Sr. M. St. Mel Kennedy, O.S.F., "The Faculty in Catholic Colleges for Women," *Catholic Educational Review*, 59 (May 1961): 289–98, reprinted in Mary J. Oates, ed., *Higher Education for Catholic Women: An Historical Anthology* (New York, 1987), 177–86, table on 178.

7. For the Sister Formation Movement, see Philip Gleason, *Contending with Modernity: Catholic Higher Education in the Twentieth Century* (New York, 1995), 226–34, and the literature cited there.

including 35 Catholic ones. The G.I. Bill gave the federal government a major role in financial support of higher education, a role expanded by the National Defense Education Act in 1958, the Higher Education Facilities Act in 1963, and by Pell Grants and other forms of student aid in the 1970s.[8]

Federal funding of university-based research, which hardly existed in the 1930s, began on a large scale during the war with defense-related contracting. Wartime experience led directly to the establishment of the National Science Foundation to coordinate the continuation of government funding of campus research; in the 1960s, the federal role as supporter of scholarly research was extended to non-scientific fields by the establishment of National Endowments for the Humanities and the Arts.[9]

Although few Catholic institutions were involved in wartime research, federal activity in higher education brought all of them out of their relative isolation and into more intensive interaction with the larger society than had been the case before 1940.[10] This naturally reinforced their assimilation to the prevailing norms of American higher education and American society generally. As they grew in enrollments and complexity, they adopted a more professional approach to such activities as admissions procedures, personnel management, and fund-raising, while also striving to improve their performance in terms of teaching and research. From the academic perspective, this was all to the good. But keeping pace with change in the secular world of higher education, however necessary and praiseworthy, could hardly avoid giving rise to some tension in regard to another imperative task of Catholic colleges—preserving their distinctive religious identity.

This tension, however, only emerged to full visibility in the 1960s. What masked it earlier? Primarily the *given* quality of the Catholicity of Catholic colleges and universities. At mid-century, the "Catholic identity" of such places was a simple social fact—so much so that the expression itself was unknown, while that which it later designated was a taken-for-granted reality. All but a handful of Catholic colleges were owned and operated by religious orders, and the exceptions were diocesan institutions. Priests, brothers, and sisters, all in religious garb, served as their chief administrators and were highly visible as faculty members. Lay faculties were overwhelmingly (probably around 90%) Catholic, and so were the student bodies. Religious devotionalism was intense, *in loco parentis* was stringently enforced in campus discipline, and no one thought of challenging the legitimacy of ecclesiastical authority. In the intellectual

---

8. In 1967, Catholic colleges received $127 million in construction grants under the Higher Education Facilities Act, but the student aid provided for in the Higher Education Act of 1972 was even more crucial to their survival. See Alice Gallin, O.S.U., *Negotiating Identity: Catholic Higher Education since 1960* (Notre Dame, Ind., 2000), 36, 78.

9. See Roger L. Geiger, *Research and Relevant Knowledge: American Research Universities Since World War II* (New York, 1993), chap. 1. By fiscal year 1969, U.S. colleges and universities were receiving more than $3.5 billion from the federal government, which amounted to approximately 17% of their total estimated expenditures for operation and construction. Lee C. Deighton, ed., *The Encyclopedia of Education*, 10 vols. (n.c., 1972), 3: 518–19.

10. For fuller discussion, see Gleason, *Contending with Modernity*, chap. 10–13.

sphere, the revival of Thomism, then at its height, bolstered Catholic confidence in their possession of a system of thought that brought reason and faith into harmony and provided the foundation for a uniquely valuable educational program.

The war and the "age of anxiety" that followed did much to restore religion to intellectual respectability in the culture at large. That reinforced the conviction, already well established among American Catholics in the 1930s, that the Church was experiencing a great intellectual and cultural revival, a veritable "Catholic Renaissance."[11] Catholic educators were likewise heartened by the postwar revival of interest in the liberal arts and its accompanying concern for curricular integration. They had long seen themselves as embattled defenders of liberal education, which they valued for its own sake and for its close connection with religion. In these circumstances, many Catholic colleges endeavored to devise curricular programs aimed at translating the integrated vision of natural and supernatural truth that was their intellectual birthright into practical courses of study. At Notre Dame, for example, a 299-page report entitled *The Curriculum of a Catholic Liberal Arts College* (1953) laid the basis for no fewer than ten curricular changes which had as their goal synthesizing the student's learning around a core of requirements in philosophy and theology.

Other currents in the postwar national culture had a more ambiguous effect on Catholics. Their anti-Communism, for example, put them safely in line with majority sentiment in the country, but it made them and their institutions suspect among the liberal intellectuals so dominant in the secular academy, especially after the demagogic Senator Joseph R. McCarthy—a Catholic and a graduate of Marquette University—emerged as the nation's leading red-baiter. By that time, many secular liberals regarded the Catholic Church as fundamentally at odds with democracy on account of its dogmatic belief system, hierarchical structure, and authoritarian mode of functioning. Paul Blanshard, the Church's leading liberal critic, made the charge explicit in his book, *American Freedom and Catholic Power* (1949), and soon followed up with another book elaborating the parallels between Catholicism and Communism as two opposing totalitarian systems.

Blanshard's polemics resonated positively with many Protestants and Jews, as well as secular liberals, because they took place against a background of intense controversy over the question of church-state separation. Catholic schools were at the center of this controversy, which erupted in earnest when a postwar proposal for federal aid to education ruled out any assistance for religious schools. It led to a series of Supreme Court decisions that established the main lines of subsequent interpretation on a stringent wall-of-separation basis. Catholics, of course, regarded rejection of their claims for aid for parochial schools as a new manifestation of historic anti-Catholic nativism. To some extent that was true, for Catholic schools had always been a sore point for nativists, and some critics of the 1940s regarded their very existence as "divisive" and for that reason un-American. However, those who asserted the constitutionality of state

---

11. For more on this topic, see Gleason, *Contending with Modernity*, chap. 5–7.

aid for parochial schools found themselves seriously embarrassed by the Church's "official teaching" that Catholicism should ideally be the religion of the state. For that position, recently restated by the prominent social progressive, Msgr. John A. Ryan, ran directly counter to a fundamental postulate of the American system.[12]

None felt this embarrassment more keenly than the growing numbers of liberal Catholic intellectuals, who were well represented on college campuses. Like the great body of their fellow Catholics, they were deeply attached to the American system, but they were also distinguished by a self-conscious commitment to the democratic values of pluralism and tolerance-for-diversity that had grown out of the nation's wartime experience. In these circumstances, they hailed the work of John Courtney Murray, S.J., who revised the accepted tradition by arguing that the American version of church-state separation was compatible with Church teaching. More broadly, they waged polemical war on "Catholic separatism" and the "siege mentality," urging their coreligionists instead to "break out of the Catholic ghetto" and engage more actively in the give-and-take of America's pluralistic society.[13]

Despite the "pluralist" rhetoric, their position was strongly assimilationist in tendency, since the liberals interpreted pluralism as calling for Catholics, Protestants, Jews, and unbelievers to join together in non-sectarian movements for the common good.[14] More obviously, the liberals' anti-ghettoism reflected their distaste for strictly Catholic organizations. This sometimes expressed itself in open ridicule of the extremes of Catholic cradle-to-grave associational life, but that did not as a rule extend to Catholic schools. Here the liberals, being loyal Catholics and on the whole committed to religious education, at first confined themselves to criticism of Catholic schools for being over-crowded and educationally deficient in other ways. But their attacks grew sharper in time, with the severest critics eventually maintaining that parochial schools had long outlived whatever usefulness they might have had in the "immigrant era," and were not even the best way to teach children their religion.[15]

Accelerating Transition, 1955–1965

It is clear in hindsight that the publication in 1955 of Msgr. John Tracy Ellis's blistering critique of American Catholic intellectual life marked the beginning of the dec-

---

12. Besides Gleason, *Contending with Modernity*, chap. 12, see John T. McGreevy, "Thinking on One's Own: Catholicism in the American Intellectual Imagination, 1928–1960," *Journal of American History*, 84 (June 1997): 97–131.

13. For anti-ghettoism, see *Catholicism in America: A Series of Articles from* The Commonweal (New York, 1953).

14. For the ambiguities of pluralism, see Philip Gleason, *Speaking of Diversity: Language and Ethnicity in Twentieth-Century America* (Baltimore, 1992), chap. 3, esp. 63–69.

15. See Mary Perkins Ryan, *Are Catholic Schools the Answer?* (New York, 1964), and Harold A. Buetow, *Of Singular Benefit: The Story of Catholic Education in the United States* (New York, 1970), 288–302.

John Tracy Ellis (Courtesy: Archives of the University of Notre Dame)

ade of accelerating transition.[16] Ellis, who shared the general perspective of the liberals, said Catholics themselves were to blame for the lamentable weakness of their record in science, scholarship, and overall cultural accomplishment. And what accounted for this failure to do justice to "the oldest, wisest and most sublime tradition of learning that the world has ever known"? The answer, Ellis said, was that Catholic scholars were insufficiently industrious and suffered from a "frequently self-imposed ghetto mentality" which kept them "from mingling as they should with their non-Catholic colleagues." By working harder and in closer contact with the world of secular learning, Catholics could draw on the riches of their heritage to help restore "religious and moral values" to their proper place in American life. Ellis's prescription was thus assimilationist in tendency, but assumed the validity of a distinctive Catholic tradition and envisioned Catholic scholars playing a correspondingly distinctive role.

Unlike earlier jeremiads on the same subject, Ellis's essay opened the floodgates to an outpouring of Catholic "self-criticism." This reaction demonstrated that a powerful undercurrent of dissatisfaction was widely shared in the Catholic intellectual community. Over time, self-criticism took on a sharper edge. American Catholics, it was said, didn't know what scholarship was; their outlook was rigid, inhibited, unable to operate in the free-wheeling mode characteristic of modern intellectual life. But the problem was not simply that too many Catholics were "dependent, submissive, pietistic, and intellectually incurious." The later critics no longer felt the same as Ellis had about the

---

16. John Tracy Ellis, "American Catholics and the Intellectual Life," *Thought*, 30 (Autumn 1955): 351–88. For discussion, see Gleason, *Contending with Modernity*, 287–96.

validity and potential of the Catholic intellectual tradition itself. On the contrary, they noted with approval that it was under severe challenge in all its "theological, structural, and historic warrants." Not even Neoscholasticism, the bedrock of American Catholic thought for over a generation, escaped unscathed; by 1960 no great daring was required to dismiss it as a deadening form of indoctrination.[17]

Actually, Ellis's faith in the tradition attracted no notice at the time. What commentators stressed was his critique and diagnosis, the assimilationist implications of which accorded with the overall trend of American Catholic life in the 1950s. In the academic world, assimilation meant acceptance of professional standards, which was, as we have seen, already well under way in Catholic institutions. John D. Donovan, one of Ellis's successors in the genre of self-criticism, put the matter plainly: the intellectual quality of Catholic colleges would improve as a new generation, formed by modern professional standards, took their places as faculty members. This "coming of age," already in process, heralded the colleges' belated emergence from their "prolonged intellectual adolescence."[18]

Academic assimilationism likewise manifested itself when Catholic educators as a group were caught up in the "pursuit of excellence" that swept the country after the Russian launching of Sputnik. More than twenty speakers treated this theme at the 1960 convention of the National Catholic Educational Association.[19] But having made a noisy public confession of their intellectual shortcomings, Catholics were not in a position to *define* academic excellence. *Research* was the key, and here the models for emulation were places like Harvard and the University of California. To younger faculty members of the sort described by Donovan, that seemed exactly right. Many of them had gotten their degrees at "big time" institutions, and had thoroughly absorbed the research ideal. But the *research ethos* is fundamentally at odds with any curricular plan that aspires to harmonize religious truth with secular knowledge, which was, of course, what the Thomistic synthesis claimed to do. That explains, for example, why the Notre Dame faculty had by 1961 become quite restive under the integrated curriculum adopted only a few years earlier. Specialists in other fields might be personally devout, but they rejected the idea that their scholarly work had to jibe with a pre-determined Catholic worldview.

Two great events in the larger world added to and accelerated the assimilative tendencies already at work in Catholic higher education—the accession of Pope John XXIII and the election of John F. Kennedy, the first Catholic to hold the office of president of the United States. Pope John's talk of *aggiornamento*, of opening the windows of the Church and letting in some fresh air, accorded beautifully with JFK's challenge to advance to "new frontiers." It was a time for looking forward, not backward. The older "Catholic Renaissance" vision, if anyone even remembered it, seemed embar-

---

17. Gleason, *Contending with Modernity*, 291–302.

18. John D. Donovan, *The Academic Man in the Catholic College* (New York, 1964), 193.

19. *National Catholic Educational Association Bulletin* (hereafter *NCEAB*), 57 (August 1960): *passim*.

rassingly parochial. But though the stream of self-criticism continued, Catholic educators never dreamed in 1960 that the coming decade would shatter the assumptions that had guided their thinking for at least two generations.

The Earthquake of the 1960s

This brings us to the second great upheaval of earthquake proportions—Vatican II and the Sixties. These are immense topics which it is impossible to discuss here in any substantive way. All I can try to do is indicate briefly how they affected the course of Catholic higher education.

Some have questioned whether Vatican II was really so important, since change was already under way. That is, of course, quite true. But the Council was nonetheless crucial because it released the built-up pressure for further change—with results like those that follow when a dam gives way releasing a wall of water that smashes everything in its path. Before the Council, ordinary Catholics believed that their Church really had the truth and would never change its teaching. But the Council not only made changes, it *legitimated change itself!*[20] This sudden and spectacular reversal gave rise to the so-called "postconciliar spirit," the more extreme representatives of which rejected their religious past with near contempt and anticipated a future of on-going radical change. Moreover the *kind of changes* introduced by the Council validated the direction American Catholics were being carried by the assimilationist tendencies of the 1950s. For the Council endorsed religious liberty, emphasized ecumenism and better relations with non-believers; promoted a more democratic people-of-God ecclesiology, qualified the hierarchical model of ecclesiastical authority with the notion of collegiality, and called for greater openness to, and more active participation in, the modern world. All this unquestionably brought the Church more nearly into line with the American values of freedom, equality, tolerance, and self-government than it had been in the days of "Tridentine" Catholicism.

This profound reorientation of its teaching, punctuated as it was by dramatic clashes between liberals and conservatives, made turbulence within the Church part and parcel of the larger explosion of the Sixties. For the spiritual confusion that marked the release of pent-up Catholic energies was more than matched by the tumult set off in American society at large by a series of shocking assassinations, racial violence, the Vietnam War and protests against it, the New Left, campus rioting, the sexual revolution, women's liberation, the drug culture, and other manifestations of social, political, and cultural radicalism. All these forms of protest were infused with an anti-traditional, anti-authoritarian—indeed, antinomian—spirit that powerfully abetted the unsettling effects of Vatican II, as the rhetoric of religious prophecy merged with that

---

20. Garry Wills stresses the importance of this point in *Bare Ruined Choirs: Doubt, Prophecy, and Radical Religion* (New York, 1972).

of revolutionary politics and gestures of ritual sacrifice accompanied anti-war demonstrations.[21] American Catholics could not help being shaken by this spiritual earthquake, and those who felt its impact most directly included two subgroups central to the life of Catholic colleges and universities—young people and religious professionals. And to make matters worse, Catholic educators simultaneously confronted a genuine fiscal crisis brought on by intensified competition from lower-priced public institutions that were expanding by leaps and bounds as the arrival on campus of the baby-boom generation sent enrollments soaring from 3 million in 1960 to 12 million in 1980.[22]

A series of controversies over academic freedom in the mid-sixties first drew public attention to the incipient revolution in Catholic higher education and prompted the most advanced thinkers to deny that the Church had any business at all running colleges and universities.[23] Not many Catholic academics went that far, but by 1968 the issue was pretty well settled as a practical matter. In the Land O'Lakes statement (1967), some two dozen leading Catholic educators and churchmen declared that Catholic universities must have "true autonomy and academic freedom"; and the inability of ecclesiastical authorities to impose effective discipline upon the hundreds of theologians who publicly repudiated the teaching of *Humanae Vitae* in 1968 demonstrated that a radically novel degree of academic freedom—even in theology—had taken root among Catholic educators. Rome, to be sure, objected, and the issue is still formally unsettled; but the practical situation in Catholic colleges and universities is entirely different from what it was as late as the 1950s.

Besides confirming freedom as an academic norm, the *Humanae Vitae* crisis reinforced the new Catholic emphasis on personal conscience because the dissenting theologians argued that married couples who were conscientious Catholics should be left free to decide for themselves whether they could licitly practice artificial birth control. This was very much in keeping with the temper of the times, for the appeal to conscience over law had acquired great moral authority in the Civil Rights Movement, where it was deployed against Jim Crow statutes. Antiwar activists, among whom Catholics played a leading role, likewise stressed the priority of conscience over laws held to be unjust, including, most pertinently for male college students, the military draft.

In addition to these points—and its overall effect in weakening the respect of American Catholics for papal and ecclesiastical authority, which Andrew Greeley has emphasized[24]—the controversy over *Humanae Vitae* hastened the complete collapse of Neoscholasticism. It had by then already lost its hegemonic place in Catholic higher education, but the dissenting theologians' unsparing attack on the role of natural-law

---

21. For an essay, originally published in 1972, that explores the interaction discussed in this paragraph and the following one, see Gleason, *Keeping the Faith*, chap. 4.

22. For the fiscal crisis, see Gallin, *Negotiating Identity*, 71–81.

23. For details, see Gleason, *Contending with Modernity*, 305–13; Gallin, *Negotiating Identity*, 58–70.

24. See Andrew M. Greeley, *The American Catholic: A Social Portrait* (New York, 1977), chap. 7.

reasoning in the Church's traditional teaching on contraception delivered the *coup de grâce* to the "perennial philosophy."

Although hardly noticed in the prevailing bedlam, the Neoscholastic meltdown was central to the "identity crisis" of Catholic higher education. For, unsatisfactory as it may appear in retrospect, Neoscholasticism's claim to reconcile religious faith with natural reason formed the cognitive cornerstone of Catholic higher education. As long as Catholic educators accepted that claim—which they did from the 1920s through the 1950s—they could rest in the conviction that their colleges and universities had a distinctive *intellectual* reason-for-being. But when the Neoscholastic system was first called into question, then all but universally abandoned by Catholics themselves, their educational enterprise was left without its own unique coign of vantage in matters intellectual. And why should a university, be it ever so good academically, exist as a *Catholic university* if its religious character did not somehow affect its mode of intellectual operation? That question, being asked in a tone of genuine puzzlement in the mid-1960s, was the crux of the identity crisis that all Catholic educators recognized by the end of the decade.[25]

Institutional changes were intimately connected with these basic shifts in ideas and outlook. The most self-consciously undertaken institutional change was the transfer of juridical authority over colleges and universities from the sponsoring religious communities to independent boards of trustees composed primarily of lay persons. Alice Gallin, O.S.U., has shown that many factors contributed to this complicated series of events, but what gave it special urgency was the fact that clerical or religious-order control made Catholic institutions vulnerable to the charge that they were pervasively "sectarian" and could not therefore receive any public funding. Legal challenges on these grounds arose just when the fiscal crisis of the late 1960s made federal aid programs crucial to the survival of Catholic colleges. Vatican II's emphasis on the dignity and role of lay people in the Church also played a significant role in justifying the shift to lay boards, as did a prominent canonist's argument that Catholic colleges had never really "belonged" to their sponsoring religious communities anyhow.[26] But it is worthy to note that the shift was unexpected when it began, and that it took place very rapidly. For though criticism of undue "clerical control" was a long-standing grievance of lay faculty members (though seldom expressed publicly before the academic freedom eruptions), not even those who were to guide the transition could have foreseen in 1965 how drastically the situation would be changed over the next few years. The change also removed almost overnight a highly visible and quite important mark of Catholic distinctiveness in higher education, for clergymen had

---

25. For the questions being asked in the mid-1960s, see my essay in Hassenger, *Shape of Catholic Higher Education*, 51–52.

26. Alice Gallin, O.S.U., *Independence and a New Partnership in Catholic Higher Education* (Notre Dame, Ind., 1996); Gallin, *Negotiating Identity*, 35–39, 42–47. The canonist mentioned was Fr. John McGrath of the Catholic University of America.

been displaced as a significant element on the governing boards of leading Protestant institutions as part of a larger process of secularization that began in the late nineteenth century.[27]

An even more important institutional change touching on the clerical dimension of Catholic higher education was the massive exodus from the priesthood and religious life, accompanied by the virtual cessation of new vocations, that began in the mid-1960s.[28] This pervasive crisis of confidence on the part of those regarded as specialists in matters spiritual delivered a body blow to the morale of the Catholic community generally. Its effects were devastating to the colleges, where the unprecedented phenomenon of wholesale resignations from the religious life was accompanied by a more diffuse sense that, in a world in crisis, religious professionals should devote themselves to work more "relevant" than delivering lectures to undergraduates of middle-class background.[29]

Between 1965 and 1990, the leading American teaching order, the Society of Jesus, lost more than a third of its numbers, falling from over 8,000 to less than 5,000. The consequences were already obvious by 1969, when it was reported that the proportion of Jesuit faculty members ranged from 32% in their smaller schools to 5% in the large universities; by the 1990s, the Jesuit presence was so exiguous on many campuses that the discussion had turned to how the Jesuit mystique could be preserved in the virtually complete absence of flesh-and-blood Jesuits.[30] Other men's communities were similarly affected. At Notre Dame, for example, only about 3% of the full-time teaching and research faculty are members of the founding religious community, the Congregation of Holy Cross.[31] The same phenomenon is so far advanced in schools founded by women religious that Melanie Morey, a sympathetic analyst of these institutions, discusses that aspect of their situation under the heading "The Disappearance of Sisters." Noting that "a mixture of ambivalence and denial" keeps college presidents and religious superiors from facing up to the problem, she adds that "something of the quality of the Emperor's New Clothes" pervades all their brave talk about a school's

27. For secularization in Protestant universities, see George M. Marsden, *The Soul of the American University: From Protestant Establishment to Established Nonbelief* (New York, 1994).

28. According to an authoritative study, 4,952 priests resigned in the years 1966–75; see Richard A. Schoenherr and Lawrence A. Young, *Full Pews and Empty Altars: Demographics of the Priest Shortage in United States Catholic Dioceses* (Madison Wisc., 1993), 206. Andrew Greeley, *The Catholic Myth: The Behavior and Beliefs of American Catholics* (New York, 1990), 218, reports that the number of seminarians fell from 46,189 in 1962 to 7,510 in 1988; and Marie Augusta Neal, *Catholic Sisters in Transition from the 1960s to the 1980s* (Wilmington, Del., 1984), 18–21, reveals an equally precipitous decline among the sisterhoods.

29. See Melanie M. Morey, "Leadership and Legacy: Is There a Future for the Past? A Study of Eight Colleges Founded by Catholic Women's Religious Congregations" (Ed.D. diss., Harvard University, 1995), 89–90, 238–41.

30. Peter McDonough, *Men Astutely Trained: A History of the Jesuits in the American Century* (New York, 1992), 5; James Tunstead Burtchaell, C.S.C., *The Dying of the Light: The Disengagement of Colleges and Universities from their Christian Churches* (Grand Rapids, Mich., 1998), 602, 609–12.

31. Information provided in 1999 by Notre Dame's office of Public Relations and Information and the office of the Indiana Province of the Congregation of Holy Cross.

preserving the distinctive character of its founding community though hardly any sisters are still teaching there.[32]

The women's colleges were in fact hit harder by the exodus than other Catholic institutions because they were more dependent on religious as teachers and administrators. The number of nuns in the United States fell from 181,000 in 1966 to 94,000 in 1993. Not only did communities of women religious lose more than half their members, those remaining were much older: in 1966, only 17% of American sisters were over 65 years of age; in 1993, more than half were.[33] These stunning shifts alone would have brought on a crisis, but they were abetted by the aforementioned loss of enthusiasm for the teaching apostolate, and by a trend away from single-sex institutions. In these circumstances, it is hardly surprising that some 42 Catholic women's colleges closed their doors by 1990; 15 others merged with, or were absorbed by, Catholic men's schools; and perhaps a dozen severed all links with the communities that founded them.[34]

Despite these losses, 118 colleges founded by women religious still exist, accounting for more than half of the 223 Catholic colleges and universities in the country. Moreover, enrollments in the women's schools grew faster in the past quarter-century than ever before.[35] What accounts for this seeming paradox? As to the number of institutions, the upgrading of junior colleges to four-year status, and the acceptance of lay students at places founded as Sister Formation schools, largely offset the closings. Most remaining Catholic women's schools also "went coed," which accounts in part for the growth in enrollments. Much more important, however, was the imaginative way the women's colleges attracted "non-traditional" students by expanding their curricular offerings, primarily in vocational fields. In the most recent phase of this development, a number of colleges founded by women religious have expanded to the point they can plausibly claim to be universities, and have gotten themselves officially designated as such.

But the continuing decline of the sisterhoods, combined with the need for more teachers to handle new subject areas and larger enrollments, means that nuns are few and far between in the schools their communities founded. Moreover, their enlarged student bodies and teaching staffs are heavily non-Catholic. As a result, these schools are now quite different *religiously* from what they were at the close of the Second Vatican Council.[36]

---

32. Melanie M. Morey, "The Way We Are: The Present Relationship of Religious Congregations of Women to the Colleges They Founded" (unpublished paper), 62–65.

33. Morey, "Leadership and Legacy," 3–4.

34. Thomas M. Landy, "A Demographic Snapshot: Catholic Higher Education, 1960–1990" (unpublished paper), 3.

35. Information on the numbers of Catholic colleges today was provided by the Association of Catholic Colleges and Universities in February, 1999; for growth in enrollments, see Landy, "Demographic Snapshot," 5–6; and Gallin, *Negotiating Identity*, 49.

36. Burtchaell, *Dying of the Light*, 661–62, analyzes the shift at the College of New Rochelle, a school particularly active in the non-traditional area.

There has also been a marked across-the-board decline in the proportion of Catholics as faculty members at Catholic institutions. However, neither its exact dimensions nor the degree of variation between different types of schools can be firmly fixed because this information is no longer routinely collected or made public. Some non-Catholics have always been present, especially at universities with a variety of professional and technical programs. Indeed, a survey of Jesuit schools in the late 1940s revealed significant variations in their representation in different departments in the arts and sciences: non-Catholics constituted 10% or less of the faculties in history, English, and modern languages, but 23% in biology and 26% in mathematics.[37] Generally speaking, however, faculties were overwhelmingly Catholic in preconciliar days. And that, according to the prevailing assumption, was as it should be, since these were, after all, *Catholic* colleges and universities, which meant that, wherever possible, Catholics should be hired as professors.

Only recently has anyone seriously questioned the general proposition that Catholics should predominate on the faculties of Catholic institutions of higher education, but the practical corollary—Catholics should therefore be preferred in hiring—eroded very rapidly in the post-conciliar era; it is now the minority position and is seen by many as an academic embarrassment. A number of factors interacted to produce this incongruous result.[38]

In the first place, Catholics-only or Catholics-first hiring was redolent of the ghettoism, defensiveness, and academic inferiority that made Catholic intellectuals squirm even before Vatican II. The Council reinforced these feelings by calling upon Catholics to involve themselves more actively in the larger world and endorsing an ecumenical outlook that had obvious implications for hiring. Moreover, ecumenism meshed beautifully with "pluralism," a prized American value that took on greater urgency than ever with the introduction of affirmative action in the early 1970s. In other words, the assimilationist quality of postconciliar religious currents worked both negatively and positively to weaken the assumptions that underlay traditional hiring practices.

Professional considerations served to reinforce the religious currents. Catholic institutions bent on achieving academic excellence naturally put a premium on that quality in hiring. This tendency was particularly marked in faculty members themselves, especially the younger cohort, which was expanding rapidly and included many who received their graduate training in leading secular universities. These younger scholars, even if Catholics themselves, were not, on the whole, disposed to give re-

---

37. Burtchaell, *Dying of the Light*, 579.

38. This discussion is based primarily on my experience and observation at Notre Dame, but see also Gregory F. Lucey, "The Meaning and Maintenance of Catholicity as a Distinctive Characteristic of American, Catholic Higher Education: A Case Study [of Marquette University]" (Ph.D. diss., University of Wisconsin-Madison, 1978), 255–56; and Joseph A. Tetlow, S.J., "The Jesuit Mission in Higher Education: Perspectives and Contexts," *Studies in the Spirituality of Jesuits*, 15–16 (November 1983–January 1984): 33.

ligion much weight in evaluating prospective colleagues. Their feelings in the matter grew stronger over time and also had greater effect. They grew stronger because more individuals were hired who shared this professional outlook, and they had greater effect because, as Catholic institutions professionalized their operating procedures, the faculty's role in governance expanded and hiring (insofar as that involved deciding among candidates for an open position) became an all-but-exclusive prerogative of departmental faculties. It was unusual for a departmental recommendation to be rejected by higher authority; and if a non-Catholic candidate was rejected, the mere suspicion that religion was involved caused indignation and nourished cynicism among the faculty.

A fortuitous practical development also helped in breaking down the old Catholics-first hiring pattern. After a quarter-century of fabulous expansion, American higher education went into a sudden slow-down in the early 1970s. All at once, academic job-seekers vastly outnumbered faculty positions open. In the resulting buyer's market—which has persisted to the present—Catholic institutions were deluged with applications from new Ph.D.'s who had glowing recommendations from Harvard, Princeton, Stanford, and other highly prestigious graduate schools. Not many of these young scholars were Catholics, and even fewer (of whatever religion, or lack of it) would, in better times, have considered taking a teaching job at a Catholic college. Their unexpected availability naturally added to the already existing pressure to hire the candidate best qualified *academically*, regardless of his or her religion. And that is now the prevailing practice: two-thirds of the Catholic colleges responding to a recent survey avow it, while fewer than one in ten reports a preference for hiring Catholics.[39]

Finally, some college presidents and their legal advisors were chary of preferential hiring of Catholics, since the open avowal of such a policy might be interpreted as "sectarian," or in violation of anti-discrimination statutes, which could in turn place the institution's eligibility for public funds in jeopardy.[40]

This combination of religious, professional, practical, and legal factors, acting over the past thirty years, has produced the situation noted above—a hollowing-out of the Catholic character of the faculty, in numbers, self-identification, and group morale. A development highly symptomatic of overall institutional slippage in religious self-confidence is the tendency to speak of a college as being "Jesuit," or "Franciscan," or "Benedictine," rather than simply describing it as "Catholic." Religious-order pride is, of course, nothing new, but the point of the newer rhetoric is to de-emphasize an institution's generically Catholic identity. A study recently conducted at three Jesuit universities shows that "Jesuit" carried generally positive connotations for those interviewed, while "Catholic" carried very negative connotations. The author went on to suggest, however, that it might be advisable for a Jesuit school to emphasize "its mission and values rather than its Jesuit and Catholic identity" since the former abstrac-

---

39. Cited in Burtchaell, *Dying of the Light*, 712.
40. Gallin, *Negotiating Identity*, 86–87.

tions could "be embraced by a plurality of people, both Catholic and non-Catholic, religious and non-religious."[41]

Efforts to Deal with the Identity Problem

As noted earlier, the existence of an "identity crisis" was widely recognized by 1970. What reactions did it prompt, and what efforts have been made to deal with the continuing identity problem? Before attempting to answer those questions, I should state that I have not researched these developments systematically, but am depending primarily on my personal experience and a general acquaintance with the literature of commentary that has grown up around them. As a result, the answers I offer must be viewed as tentative, as well as being sketchy and schematic.

To say that the term "identity crisis" had become a cliché by 1970 does not mean that all observers viewed the situation negatively.[42] On the contrary, there were many who believed that what was happening to Catholic colleges was a good thing—a travail of liberation from which they would emerge better academically and more truly Catholic than ever. Other observers, while willing to grant that changes from the old system were overdue, were made uneasy by the parallels with what had happened to mainline Protestant institutions which had become effectively secularized by around 1900.[43] But the late 1960s were hectic days for all educators, and "confusion" was probably the term used most often to describe the Catholic situation.

By the 1970s, however, administrators of Catholic colleges realized that the religious identity of their institutions needed explicit *reaffirmation*. That recognition resulted in the self-conscious drawing up of "mission statements" (documents previously rare, if not non-existent in Catholic institutions of higher education) which included such reaffirmations. At Notre Dame, for example, a series of institutional self-studies, beginning in 1973 and repeated at ten-year intervals, listed preservation of the university's Catholic identity as its first and most important priority. Corresponding to those adopted by individual colleges and universities were collective declarations

---

41. The quotation is from an unpublished study (dated Jaunary 31, 2000) done for the Association of Jesuit Colleges and Universities. It is based on 31 interviews with faculty, administrators, professional staff, and students. See also Burtchaell, *Dying of the Light*, 622, 628; and Morey, "Leadership and Legacy," 190–91.

42. For a variety of assessments, see David J. O'Brien, *From the Heart of the American Church: Catholic Higher Education and American Culture* (Maryknoll, N.Y., 1994), esp. chap. 5–6; and the essays collected in Theodore M. Hesburgh, C.S.C., ed., *The Challenge and Promise of a Catholic University* (Notre Dame, Ind., 1994).

43. Philip Gleason, "Freedom and the Catholic University," *NCEAB*, 65 (November 1968): 21–29, emphasizes similarities between Protestant and Catholic developments; Alice Gallin, O.S.U., "American Catholic Higher Education: An Experience of Inculturation," in William M. Shea and Daniel Van Slyke, eds., *Trying Times: Essays on Catholic Higher Education in the 20th Century* (Atlanta, Ga., 1999), 110–17, emphasizes differences.

such as "The Catholic University in the Modern World," a statement issued by the International Federation of Catholic Universities in 1972.[44] These reaffirmations of purpose and identity constitute the first identifiable actions taken to deal with the identity problem. I will call this the *official response*, which, though formalistic, is quite important by reason of its public nature and symbolic value.

A second type, which might be called the *progressive response*, was not devised specifically for the purpose of dealing with the identity problem. I am thinking here of the emphasis on the ethical dimension of religious belief, particularly Catholic social doctrine, which emerged as a purposeful educational thrust in the late 1970s and has since inspired many curricular and extra-curricular programs in Catholic colleges. This approach is clearly related to Vatican II's teaching on the relationship of the Church to the modern world, to the social concerns of the 1960s, and to liberation theology and other recent currents of religious thought. Those who champion it do so because they are convinced it flows organically from the Church's teaching, and therefore represents what Catholics really ought to be doing in education. But they also perceive that its general adoption would provide a new *raison d'être* for Catholic colleges and thereby solve the identity problem. Thus in introducing a new program of this sort at Notre Dame in 1999, its director pointed out that, as a Catholic university, Notre Dame "should have programs that promote its Catholic identity such as the Catholic Social Tradition concentration."[45]

The third is the *conservative response*, which stresses the need for a reassertion of traditional Catholic teaching. As in the case of its progressive counterpart, it embraces a wide range of positions from moderate to extreme. It manifests itself in the formation of groups like the Fellowship of Catholic Scholars and the Cardinal Newman Society for the Preservation of Catholic Higher Education, and in the establishment of new institutions such as Christendom College in Virginia that make a special point of their doctrinal orthodoxy.[46] The conservatives support, and take encouragement from, Roman efforts carried out since the early 1970s to establish closer ecclesiastical supervision over the teaching of theology and over Catholic higher education in general. In fact, the Cardinal Newman Society claims credit for letting Rome know that not all American Catholic educators endorse the position taken by the

---

44. For the Notre Dame documents, see *Notre Dame Report*, 3 (December 14, 1973); ibid., 12 (December 24, 1982); and ibid., 22 (June 18, 1993); for a case study of the mission statement of the College of the Holy Cross, see O'Brien, *Heart of the Church*, chap. 7; for IFCU's 1972 statement and other church documents up to and including *Ex Corde Ecclesiae* in 1990, see Alice Gallin, O.S.U., ed., *American Catholic Higher Education: Essential Documents, 1967–1990* (Notre Dame, Ind., 1992).

45. *Notre Dame Observer*, 25 February 1999; for the approach in general, see David M. Johnson, ed., *Justice and Peace Education: Models for College and University Faculty* (Maryknoll N.Y., 1986); and O'Brien, *Heart of the Church*, chap. 10.

46. Mary Jo Weaver, "Self-Consciously Countercultural: Alternative Catholic Colleges," in Weaver and R. Scott Appleby, eds., *Being Right: Conservative Catholics in America* (Bloomington, Ind., 1995), chap. 12.

"establishment" Association of Catholic Colleges and Universities, which it regards as unacceptably compromising.[47]

Roman intervention has certainly buttressed the conservative response. Moreover, it provides a salutary religious counter-pressure to the assimilationist and secularizing forces acting so powerfully on Catholic colleges and universities. In so doing, it has *required* Catholic educators to deal with the identity question in more concrete terms than they might otherwise have been disposed to do. On the other hand, the ten-year struggle over Rome's determination to establish direct juridical authority over Catholic colleges, ostensibly in order to achieve the goals set forth in *Ex Corde Ecclesiae* (1990), has undoubtedly reinforced the negative connotations associated with the word "Catholic." Indeed, one could hardly ask for a better illustration of "the *You must obey!* mentality . . . so commonly attributed to Catholic institutions" and so offensive to American academics.[48] Moreover, it is yet to be seen whether the loyalty oaths and mandates for Catholic theologians that Rome insists upon can actually be implemented without serious damage to the academic and legal standing of Catholic universities. Insofar as the conservative response is identified with pressure from Rome, the results are thus quite mixed.

A fourth response to the identity question comprises specialized programs aimed at promoting the study and teaching of the Catholic religion in itself and in its relation to the historical past and to issues of the present day. "Catholic Studies Programs" represent the most widely applied example of these efforts to address the intellectual dimension of Catholic identity in a systematic way. Formal undergraduate programs in Catholic Studies did not begin to appear until the 1990s, but are multiplying rapidly. A feature story in the *National Catholic Reporter* (16 October 1998) described a dozen or so, and a number of others have gotten under way since then. Most offer course sequences that constitute a collegiate major or minor, but two or three also exist at the graduate level. Another project of a somewhat similar nature is "Collegium," which organizes summer institutes for young faculty members interested in exploring the intellectual dimensions of their Catholic faith and its relation to their work as teachers and researchers. There are also a few specialized centers to encourage research and publication in Catholic history and theology, such as those at Boston College, Georgetown, and Notre Dame. In fact, there are two at Notre Dame: the Cushwa Center for the Study of American Catholicism, founded by Jay Dolan in 1975, and the newly-established Erasmus Center, which encourages work related to the Catholic intellectual tradition from early Christian times to the present. Another project still in the planning stage looks toward the establishment of a free-standing institute along the lines of Princeton's Institute for Advanced Study, but devoted to research in the Catholic tradition of learning.

---

47. For the Cardinal Newman Society's position, see the July 1997 issue of its newsletter, *The Turnaround*; for a general account of Roman interventions, see Gallin, *Negotiating Identity*, chap. 6.

48. Quotation from Morey, "Leadership and Legacy," 191.

Moderates among both progressives and conservatives can support initiatives like these, which are a source of encouragement to all for whom the preservation of Catholic identity is a prized objective. The same could be said of grass roots movements, such as one that emerged at Notre Dame in the early 1990s (and seems to have run its course), in which concerned members of the faculty, Catholic and non-Catholic alike, organized a series of discussions of the university's religious identity and how it might best be manifested and preserved.

But encouraging as developments like these may be, and however much one may endorse what I have called the official, progressive, or conservative responses to the problem, the older pattern—"Catholic identity" as it existed before anyone thought of calling it that—is, in my opinion, gone for good. For that older pattern envisaged the entire experience of learning taking place within a cognitive framework based on religious faith and articulated by a philosophical system that harmonized faith and reason. While reality may never have conformed to the vision, and tension between the two increased sharply after 1955, the crisis of the Sixties shattered the social reality and intellectual assumptions on which the vision itself rested. There are, to be sure, those who still hold the older view, and institutions that try to realize it, but as the official consensus position of the enterprise as a whole, it is no longer operative. That does not mean Catholic institutions will inevitably follow the path of complete secularization so many formerly Protestant universities did. It does, however, suggest that those who believe in Catholic higher education face a severe challenge and would do well to overcome their ideological differences and work together to realize the ideal in new form.

Perspectives on the Nineteenth-Century Diocesan Seminary in the United States

Joseph M. White

Through his major works, *Immigrant Church: New York's Irish and German Catholics* (1975), *Catholic Revivalism: The American Experience, 1830–1900* (1977), and *American Catholic Experience: A History from Colonial Times to the Present* (1985) Jay Dolan has gone to the heart of the nineteenth-century experience of immigrant Catholics. The many dimensions of their *experience*—a key word in two of the titles above—are suggested in the chapter headings of *American Catholic Experience* with such topics as parish, neighborhood, Catholic ethos, handing on the Faith, and schools among others. His approach, departing from the previous ways of portraying Catholicism, reveal the religious and social dimensions shaping the lives of ordinary Catholics and their institutions.

The needs of immigrants shaped the development of American Catholic institutions in the nineteenth century. These institutions—parishes with their schools, academies, colleges, hospitals, orphanages—enjoyed a high visibility wherever Catholics settled in substantial numbers. Another Catholic institution, the diocesan seminary, likewise developed through the nineteenth century. It did not have the same high profile as other Catholic institutions since a seminary was not to be found in every substantial community of Catholics. As treated in this essay, the diocesan seminary in the United States during the nineteenth century was heir to the seminary tradition of the Council of Trent as adapted to the circumstances of an immigrant Church. In the same century, Roman authority began to depart from Tridentine practices related to the seminary and took some initiatives in the internal life of the U.S. Church that touched on the role of the diocesan seminary. Through the century the diocesan seminary was gradually transformed.

The Catholic Seminary Tradition

By the nineteenth century, as the immigrant Church was developing in the United States, the tradition of the diocesan seminary had been in operation since the Council of Trent's seminary decree, *Cum Adolescentium Aetas,* of 1563. This landmark decree enjoins each bishop to sponsor a *seminarium* (seed bed) or seminary at his official church, the cathedral, to prepare poor youth as priests of his diocese. The seminary is thereby attached to an existing institution, the cathedral—a very public place. Its students were to participate in the cathedral's liturgical life—bringing them in view of the faithful who would be aware of the formation of future priests. The cathedral canons were to have responsibilities for directing the seminary under the bishop's authority. Without providing a detailed program of studies, the decree expects poor young males to receive moral training, a general education, and instruction in the tasks of ministry. Seminary formation was not made a requirement for ordination thereby allowing affluent priesthood candidates recourse to theological studies at universities.[1] Despite the decree's limitations, such as not addressing the training of priests belonging to religious orders, it signaled a turning away from informal practices of preparing candidates for diocesan priesthood and implanted the ideal that diocesan priests required formal training for ministry.

One of the decree's greatest strengths is its brevity that allows the details concerning length of studies and the content of learning to be left to the bishop's determination. No Roman congregation then existed or would exist until 1915 to devise a program of studies, establish its length in terms of years, or investigate compliance with its regulations. Instead, given the responsibility assigned to the bishop, the primacy of the local church's needs stands out as a central characteristic of the diocesan seminary.

From Trent until the nineteenth century, the diocesan seminary passed through more than two centuries in which influential figures set precedents at various times and places that guided practices of clerical formation. Through this process, the Tridentine seminary tradition demonstrated its ability to adapt to changing needs. A major influence on the course of seminary history was the French School of Spirituality arising in the seventeenth century. Its major figures, Pierre de Bérulle, Charles de Condren, Vincent de Paul, and Jean Jacques Olier, developed a spirituality for diocesan priests, stressing personal self-denial and mental prayer focusing on Christ's life. By thus conforming to Christ, the seminarian prepared for the priest's role of imparting grace through the ministry of the sacraments. To staff diocesan seminaries throughout France, the French School produced clerical communities such as Olier's company of diocesan priests, the Society of St. Sulpice (Sulpicians), formed in 1641, and Vincent de Paul's Congregation of the Mission (Vincentians), founded in 1625. The French School's legacy that has influenced the entire Church is the primacy assigned to spiritual formation in preparing candidates for priesthood.

---

1. The text of the seminary decree is available in English translation in Henry J. Schroeder, ed., *Canons and Decrees of the Council of Trent* (Rockford, Ill.: Tan Books, 1978), 175.

The Diocesan Seminary in America

The introduction of the diocesan seminary to the United States began the process of adapting its Tridentine design to the needs of an emerging Church. The opening of the first diocesan seminary in the country reveals the interest of a group other than the local bishop.[2] In 1791, four Sulpician priests opened the first diocesan seminary in the United States at Baltimore, the seat of the country's first diocese. They did so at their own initiative in order to escape the effects of the French Revolution and with the approval of Baltimore's Bishop John Carroll. An initial adaptation related to the way the seminary was organized. Because seminarians were few, the Sulpicians, who had no tradition of lay education, opened an affiliated lay college in 1805 to secure tuition revenue for the seminary's support. Sulpicians initially sponsored Mt. St. Mary's College at Emmitsburg, Maryland, started in 1808, as a minor seminary to educate boys in the classics as preparation for theological studies at their Baltimore seminary. Soon this seminary had to be adapted to sponsor a lay college and added theological instruction for older seminarians who served as part-time teachers of younger students.

In addition to Sulpicians, Vincentians arrived from Rome under the leadership of Felix de Andreis and Joseph Rosati to open St. Mary of the Barrens Seminary in 1818 at Perryville, Missouri in response to the invitation of the local bishop. Like the Sulpicians, the Vincentians had no tradition of conducting lay education but expanded the aims of their seminary to include a lay college by 1820 to sustain clerical formation.

Through the first half of the nineteenth century, bishops took seriously their responsibility to conduct seminaries. In the thirty-one dioceses established across the country up to 1851, most bishops established or attempted to establish their own seminaries. At their second Provincial Council of Baltimore in 1833, the bishops reminded themselves of the duty of doing so in conformity to the decree of the Council of Trent. In their attempts to form seminaries, they tried various institutional models. With funds scarce, a bishop might train seminarians in his own residence, at the cathedral rectory, or combined with a Catholic school for lay students. The number of seminarians remained low. Most were immigrants themselves recruited from European seminaries. The small scale of these local seminaries is revealed in the 1842 report of Canon Josef Salzbacher, a representative of the *Leopoldinen Stiftung* of Vienna who toured the United States on behalf of this mission society. He counted twenty-two diocesan seminaries then in operation collectively enrolling 277 seminarians for an average of 12.5 seminarians per seminary.[3]

---

2. The narrative of seminary developments is drawn from Joseph M. White, *The Diocesan Seminary in the United States: A History from the 1780s to the Present* (Notre Dame: University of Notre Dame Press, 1989; the research and writing of this work was sponsored by the Cushwa Center for the Study of American Catholicism when Jay P. Dolan was director with funding from the Lilly Endowment.

3. Josef Salzbacher, *Meine Reise nach Nord-Amerika im Jahre 1842* (Vienna, 1845), 358.

By the 1840s, the average diocesan seminary, then, was small, local in scope, enrolling immigrant seminarians, and resting on a shaky financial basis thereby reflecting the circumstances of the immigrant Church. In some ways these efforts were acts of hope. Though few students came from local Catholic communities, there was always the possibility that some might aspire to the priesthood and enroll in the seminary. Uneven supplies of funds, seminarians, and priests trained for seminary faculties meant that few of these seminaries survived beyond mid-century. Founding numerous small seminaries had its critics. A German born, university-trained seminary educator, Father Michael Heiss, writing from Milwaukee where he later became archbishop, noted in 1853 the "antipathy" of bishops against any united action to support seminaries. "Each one wants a seminary in his own diocese, and for this very reason, none amounts to anything decent. In my opinion a good seminary would be possible only if, at the very least, the Bishops of a province would unite and build a common seminary."[4] In response to Heiss, it might be said, the prevailing system was not tidy or even rational, but it conformed to the Tridentine tradition that forming diocesan clergy was a local affair.

For Heiss and other critics, a change of attitude was already under way. Instead of each diocese having its own seminary, the more realistic approach was for larger dioceses with financial resources to develop seminaries to train students of several dioceses. When the bishops of the United States met for the First Plenary Council of Baltimore in 1852, (actually their eighth national council following the seven provincial councils of Baltimore, 1829–1849) they framed a seminary decree that reflected the change in episcopal thinking since their Second Provincial Council of Baltimore in 1833. They urged the founding of diocesan seminaries, but if this was not possible, then the bishops of an ecclesiastical province should cooperate to form a provincial seminary. The bishops reaffirmed this ideal again at their Second Plenary Council of Baltimore in 1866.

The new approach to seminaries of the 1850s provided a context to the founding of what twentieth-century seminary educators commonly call 'freestanding' seminaries. These seminaries were not attached to other enterprises such as a lay college, the bishop's household, or the local cathedral. At leading sees, the new type of seminary was founded on substantial campuses that separated their resident communities from nearby urban life—hardly in the spirit of the Tridentine decree's ideal of locating the seminary at the cathedral. Examples of the new type of seminary arose around the country: Mt. St. Mary's of the West Seminary, Cincinnati (1851); St. Francis de Sales Seminary, Milwaukee (1856); and St. Joseph's Provincial Seminary, Troy, New York (1864–1896). In 1855, the Sulpicians in downtown Baltimore discontinued their lay college to devote their resources exclusively to clerical formation at St. Mary's and St. Charles Minor Seminary. In downtown Philadelphia, the diocese sponsored the modest St. Charles Borromeo Seminary devoted exclusively to clerical formation since

---

4. Quoted in M. Mileta Ludwig, *Right Hand Glove Uplifted: A Biography of Archbishop Michael Heiss* (New York: Pageant Press, 1968), 202.

Mt. Saint Mary's of the West Seminary in Cincinnati with its nineteenth-century buildings located in the city's Price Hill neighborhood. (Original print in Michael J. Kelly and James M. Kirwin, History of Mt. Saint Mary's Seminary of the West, *Cincinnati, 1894)*

1838. In 1871, the seminary moved into a magnificent building on a park-like campus outside the city at Overbrook. Unlike earlier diocesan seminaries, all these freestanding seminaries housed substantial communities of seminarians.

Through the same period in a further adaptation of the Tridentine concept of the diocesan seminary, male religious orders and congregations got into the act. Such Benedictine monasteries now known as St. Vincent Archabbey, Latrobe, Pennsylvania (1846), St. John's Abbey, Collegeville, Minnesota (1857), and St. Meinard Archabbey, in southern Indiana (1854) sponsored seminaries training diocesan seminarians for local dioceses in the multi-dimensional context of a monastic community whose activities included lay education, farming, book publishing, and ministry in local parishes. The Vincentians, who had opened a seminary with a lay college at Perryville, Missouri earlier in the century, continued that tradition at a different location with their St. Vincent College, at nearby Cape Girardeau, from 1859 to 1894, and at Our Lady of the Angels Seminary, Niagara College, Niagara Falls, New York opening in 1863. Franciscans sponsored a seminary at their St. Bonaventure College opening in 1859 at Allegheny, New York.

All this flexibility of institutional arrangements reflected creativity as American church leaders dealt with the challenges of providing trained ministers to serve the immigrant Church. In doing so, they adapted the Tridentine tradition of the seminary to local needs.

Another aspect of the Tridentine tradition of the diocesan seminary is local determination of the content of clerical learning. In the U.S. Church the great demand for priests required that they be educated quickly to serve immigrant flocks that had limited need for highly intellectual clergy. As early as 1813, before the inundation of immigrants from Catholic Europe, founding Bishop John Carroll favored conferring holy orders on "as many as can be trusted to receive them, tho they may not have studied all the Treatises of Divinity, provided they know the obvious and general principles of moral Theology. . . ."[5] Bishop John England in the Charleston of the 1820s and 1830s ordained men with incomplete studies, sent them on missionary travels around his vast diocese encompassing the Carolinas and Georgia, and then recalled them periodically for periods of study under his direction. The overwhelming pastoral demands on priests, particularly in urban areas, resulted in Archbishop John Hughes of New York adopting a totally pragmatic view of priesthood. In an 1858 report he outlined the qualities of a useful priest of his archdiocese: "If any one looks for extraordinary eloquence in the pulpit, or immense erudition, or able writers among the Clergy of New York, he may be prepared for much disappointment." Their time was devoted to the ministry of sacraments, stating "if there be a few, who are capable of eloquence in the pulpit, or able to write in defence of religion, they neglect their capacity, and, on the other hand, are but little distinguished for their zeal, or laboriousness in the duties of the Ministry."[6] It is not surprising then that Father William Barry, the young rector of Cincinnati's seminary remarked in 1861: "We have known cases of persons having been ordained after their first year's theology; and some have graduated in ecclesiastical science, after an extensive course of six months."[7] This brevity of seminary studies prompted Bishop Martin Spalding of Louisville in the 1850s to advocate formation of the American College at the great Catholic University at Louvain, Belgium to prepare Europeans to become priests in America, noting "Our studies in America are woefully below the European standard, and a few good missionaries educated in Belgium scattered through our various Dioceses would leaven the whole mass."[8] By the 1850s, in fact, seminary studies were improving, albeit slowly, as most freestanding seminaries offered three or four years of philosophical and theological study. However, nothing prevented a bishop from withdrawing a seminarian before completing his studies and ordaining him because of an urgent need for priests.

The Bedini Visit

In view of the primacy of local responsibility for the diocesan seminary, where was Roman authority in these issues? In the tradition of Tridentine Catholicism, Rome was

---

5. John Carroll to John Grassi, Baltimore, 30 November 1813, in Thomas O'Brien Hanley, *John Carroll Papers* (Notre Dame: University of Notre Dame Press, 1976), 3:243–244.

6. Henry J. Browne, ed., "The Archdiocese of New York a Century Ago: A Memoir of Archbishop Hughes, 1838–1858," *Historical Records and Studies,* 49–50 (1950), 163.

7. William J. Barry, "Catholic Education in the United States," *Brownson's Quarterly Review* (Third New York Series) 2 (January 1861), 58.

8. John D. Sauter, *The American College of Louvain (1857–1898)* (Louvain: Publications Universitaires de Louvain, 1959), 19.

Archbishop Gaetano Bedini, 1806–1864.
(Original copy in Archives of the
Archdiocese of Cincinnati)

far removed from these and other local church matters. However, an intervention of the Holy See in U.S. Church affairs took place that touched on the training of priests. In 1853, the secretary of the Congregation of Propaganda Fide announced to the U.S. bishops that the nuncio to Brazil, Archbishop Gaetano Bedini, would visit the United States but left the purpose of his visit vague. In June 1853, Archbishop Bedini arrived in New York City for his U.S. tour along with a side trip to Canada, lasting until his departure in February 1854 for Rome, not Brazil. His visit was the first time a representative of the Holy See came to look over the Church in the U.S. Moreover, the visit was Propaganda's response to complaints about the American bishops from letter writers in the United States. In his formal instructions, Bedini was charged to look for abuses, tactfully call them to the bishops' attention, and to report on conditions that he found. He was also to sound out the United States government on the possibility of establishing diplomatic relations.

Had the country's bishops been consulted beforehand, they might have persuaded Propaganda officials not to send Bedini at this time. The early 1850s were peak years for Catholic immigrant arrivals from Europe. In reaction, nativist feelings were running high as expressed in the anti-immigrant and anti-Catholic American or Know Nothing Party that opposed unlimited immigration. Demonstrations accompanied Bedini's visits to Catholic communities in major cities on his tour. In the custom of the times, he was often 'burned in effigy.' The high point of this unrest occurred in Cincinnati where on Christmas night of 1853, demonstrators marched on Archbishop John B. Purcell's home where Bedini was staying. In the melee with the police near Purcell's home, one protester was killed, two policemen and fourteen protesters were injured, and sixty were arrested. Bedini left the country in February 1854 annoyed that the U.S. government had not taken better care of an accredited ambassador, albeit to another country, and personally hurt that the U.S. bishops had not publicly defended the visit. From their point of view, the visit was a bad idea, as Archbishop Peter Kenrick of St. Louis stated, "a blunder in every point of view."[9] The bishops had not been consulted about the visit, and in the climate of the times, how could they honestly defend the indefensible.

Bedini's lengthy report on his tour submitted to Roman authorities remains one of the most interesting contemporary views of the U.S. Church in the nineteenth century. The report concluded with recommendations. A major one was the establishment of diplomatic relations with the United States—a matter not likely to be pursued—and not achieved until 1984. Another major recommendation related to the education of clergy. Bedini had described the largely immigrant clergy in terms of their national groups, pointing out the obvious fact that "For the most part they are European and not American, and each one has the customs and prejudices of his own nation." He did not conclude from the situation that there was a need to develop an American clergy by improving seminaries then existing in the United States. Unimpressed with the seminaries visited on his tour, he found them "well managed, but all of them labor under the burden of their vast dioceses." Tending to exaggerate, he recommended a solution to U.S. clergy issues: "The single most important thing, that would satisfy every desire, achieve every purpose and would give the greatest enthusiasm to America" would be an American College in Rome. He foresaw many advantages in a college: (1) "Roman Catholic spirit would be assured among priests and people," citing the record of other national colleges in Rome as proof. (2) The college would "facilitate and encourage vocations to the priesthood" because the number of American seminaries was not sufficient and the seminarians attending them returned to their homes during the summer, a practice "sometimes fatal" to their perseverance in the seminary. While eliminating the latter danger, a Roman college would educate students at a lower cost than seminaries in the United States. (3) The college would provide "a wider, more complete and more solid education to the American clergy," citing the unsatisfactory scholastic exercises that he witnessed at American seminaries. (4) The college would be the logical place to prepare "successors" of the many U.S. bishops. Their proper education lay in Rome "where the means, the resources, the occasions for perfecting oneself in learning, in spirit and zeal abound." As if the previous reason was not strong enough he reiterated (5) that "By means of this College, the Holy See will be able to know the American Clergy better in its representatives, and thus can makes its selection [of bishops] with greater confidence." Bedini cited a less persuasive reason but one perhaps very compelling to him; he desired that the visit of the

---

9. Peter Kenrick to John B. Purcell, St. Louis, 9 February 1854, Cincinnati Papers, University of Notre Dame Archives.

"first Pontifical Nuncio" to America be vindicated by some result more important than the "ashes of effigies which were burnt to mock him."[10]

Before formulating his proposal for an American College, one wonders if he had a serious discussion of the subject with any U.S. bishops during his tour. Since the 1790s, some bishops had been sending a few American seminarians to the Urban College of the Propaganda in Rome. Several American alumni of the Urban College were destined to become bishops in the United States. In recommending the formation of an American College in Rome, Bedini was preaching to the converted. It was already a policy of Pope Pius IX to encourage the formation of national colleges such as the French, Irish, Latin American, and Polish colleges established in his pontificate in order to reinforce Roman loyalties.

The next step, as Robert F. McNamara recounts in his definitive work, *The American College Rome, 1855–1955,* occurred later in 1854 when Pope Pius IX met the delegation of four U.S. bishops attending the solemn definition of the dogma of the Immaculate Conception. He surprised them by expressing his desire for an American College in Rome. The bishops had mixed reactions, but any of their misgivings were irrelevant. In a letter to U.S. archbishops in February 1855, the prefect of Propaganda, Cardinal Giacomo Fransoni wrote that the pope "had reached the conclusion that the project should be recommended; and he has willed by this letter of the Sacred Congregation to urge Your Grace to enter into consultation with the other bishops for the erection of the proposed college."[11]

The consultation among bishops at their forthcoming provincial councils around the country in 1855 revealed the mixed reception to the pope's college. The bishops of the Baltimore province under the influence of Archbishop Francis Kenrick enthusiastically endorsed the college's founding and proposed a fund-raising plan. The bishops of the St. Louis and New Orleans ecclesiastical provinces expressed appreciation for the idea of the college, but the St. Louis bishops said it was too early to open it, and the New Orleans bishops said they did not have the means to contribute to it. Apparently misreading the pope's intentions and thinking the issue of the American College was an open question, the Cincinnati province's bishops stated their outright opposition to the college. After all, these midwestern bishops had just designated the new Cincinnati seminary as their provincial seminary. The New York province's bishops through Archbishop Hughes pledged a rather modest gift of $5,000 for the proposed college. The latter also polled the country's other archbishops and reported "Not one is able to give immediate or direct practical encouragement in the way of supplying funds or students."[12] The background to the lack of interest may be

---

10. James Connelly, *The Visit of Archbishop Gaetano Bedini to the United States of America, June 1853–February 1854* (Roma: Università Gregoriana, 1954), 244–247.

11. Quoted in Robert F. McNamara, *The American College in Rome, 1855–1863* (Rochester: Christopher Press, 1956), 17.

12. Quoted in McNamara, *American College,* 32.

explained by the consul of the Papal States in New York City, the French layman Louis Binsse, a formidable collector of ecclesiastical gossip. He reported to Rome that indifference to the proposed college was based on the widely held view in the United States concerning priest-alumni of the Urban College that "there is no particular excellence among those who have studied at Rome over those educated here."[13]

Aided with the funds from lay donors in New York and Baltimore, Archbishop Bedini, by then secretary of the Congregation of Propaganda Fide and no doubt still remembering those burnt effigies, pushed relentlessly for the college's opening. After the former Visitation Sisters convent on the Via dell'Umiltà was purchased and remodeled as its home, Archbishop Bedini opened the American College there on December 8, 1859, with only twelve students on hand from eight U.S. dioceses. The students were to reside at the college while taking classes at the Urban College of the Propaganda. The opening was just the beginning of an ongoing struggle to maintain the college through the 1860s in face of the indifference of the U.S. bishops who supplied it with few students and limited funds. The fear that the college might be closed when the world's bishops were due to meet in 1870 for Vatican Council I energized a fundraising campaign in 1868 and 1869 that 'saved' the college, but its results fell far short of providing the endowment that the Congregation of Propaganda demanded. Without an endowment, the Propaganda was unwilling to transfer ownership of the college to the U.S. bishops who would subsequently govern it. Until then, Propaganda controlled the college. At the time, given the lack of enthusiasm for the college, Pope Pius IX told Father De Neve, the founding rector of the American College at Louvain that opened in 1857, "We both founded an American College, but you succeeded better than I did."[14] The issue of the endowment would be superseded in the 1880s by the concern that a hostile Italian government would confiscate the college as property of the Holy See along with other church properties. In this context Pope Leo XIII granted the college a pontifical charter in 1884, and it thereafter was under the control of a board of U.S. bishops. By century's end, more bishops had overcome an earlier episcopal coolness toward the college and were enrolling a larger number of their seminarians. The college had thereby finally achieved a certain legitimacy for the U.S. bishops despite the Catholic Church's longer tradition affirmed in the Tridentine seminary decree that training diocesan priests was the responsibility of the local bishop.

Seminary Issues in the 1880s

While the founding of the American College represented one kind of Roman intervention related to the training of American diocesan priests and the U.S. bishops

---

13. Quoted in John Peter Marschall, "Francis Patrick Kenrick, 1851–1863: The Baltimore Years" (Ph.D. diss., Catholic University of America, 1965), 281.

14. Quoted in McNamara, *American College,* 157.

response, the Congregation of Propaganda Fide intervened with a different response in the 1880s. By then, the U.S. Church was marked with the continual struggles between bishops and their diocesan priests. Since the full weight of canon law was not in effect in a missionary country such as the United States, there were no canonical parishes, just 'missions,' as parish churches were then called, and diocesan priests had no canonical rights proper to parish clergy. Priests were assigned to a 'mission' at the command of their bishop and could be reassigned at any time. Against their bishops' frequently arbitrary actions, aggrieved priests appealed regularly to Roman authorities. This crisis of mutual confidence of bishops and their priests created a corresponding concern among Propaganda officials.

To address these and other issues facing the U.S. Church, the Congregation of Propaganda ordered the U.S. bishops to hold a plenary council. Roman authority had another reason to be concerned about the U.S. church. Gerald Fogarty proposes as the "determinative" reason for convening a council: Roman authority "wished to test the loyalty of the American bishops, since many had opposed the definition of papal infallibility" at the Vatican Council of 1870.[15] Unlike previous plenary councils, Propaganda not only ordered a council but summoned a delegation of U.S. bishops to come to Rome to draft the council's agenda.

In preparation for the meeting of Propaganda officials and the U.S. bishops, one from each ecclesiastical province, the Jesuit theologian, Cardinal Johannes Franzelin, one of the cardinals of Propaganda, prepared a massive *ponenza* or memorandum with allied documents. Franzelin's document analyzes the problems of the U.S. Church from the Roman perspective and identifies its two major difficulties as discipline and debts. The discipline issue relates to priests' behavior that was worsening with the numerous bishop-priest conflicts generating unfavorable publicity wherever they occurred "to the great joy of the enemies of Catholicism." Debts, of course, resulted from the Church's rapid institutional expansion in the 'bricks-and-mortar' era of American Catholic life. Franzelin apparently did not question the need for this spending only the fact that priests were handling money through fund-raising by sponsoring lotteries, fairs, and picnics.

The problems of the U.S. Church's unruly priesthood in Franzelin's view could be traced to inadequate seminary training. He subjected American diocesan seminaries to a severe appraisal. From his perspective, there were few of them. He noted only four— St. Mary's in Baltimore, St. Charles Borromeo in Philadelphia, St. Francis de Sales in Milwaukee, and St. Joseph's in Troy, New York. The Cincinnati seminary was temporarily closed because of that archdiocese's bankruptcy, and Mt. St. Mary's Seminary at Emmitsburg, Maryland was near closing because of finances. The six seminaries operated by Benedictines, Vincentians, and Franciscans for the training of diocesan priests

---

15. Gerald Fogarty, *The Vatican and the American Hierarchy from 1870 to 1965* (Wilmington, Del.: Michael Glazier, 1985), 27–28.

Saint Mary's College, Saint Mary's Chapel, Saint Mary's Seminary, Baltimore in the early nineteenth century. (Courtesy: the Sulpician Archives Baltimore)

were not even mentioned. The cardinal recommended compliance with the Tridentine decree that dioceses should sponsor seminaries, not recognizing that this approach had been tried and found wanting decades ago. He also recommended that if a diocese lacked a seminary then each ecclesiastical province should have one. Of the existing seminaries, Franzelin concluded that their two principal defects were the brevity of the course of studies and the seminarians' departure for summer vacations at home. According to Franzelin, the major seminary's studies of three or four years reflected the American view that a good priest did not need much learning. As for the seminarians' vacations, "nothing does more harm" than letting them go home. Franzelin tended to overgeneralize about seminarians' vacations, stating the young men were "indulged by all" and made "continual journeys on horseback, went hunting, and, what is worse, went to beach resorts, dressed entirely as laymen." These fun times caused them "to lose the love of study that they had and all idea of ecclesiastical spirit."[16]

In their conference with three cardinals of Propaganda, Cardinals Giovanni Fransoni, the prefect, Johannes Franzelin, and Lodovico Jacobini, the Vatican Secretary of State, in November 1883, eleven U.S. bishops dealt with the questions raised in the Franzelin document. A major point of disagreement was the cardinals' proposal for the construction of villas to house seminarians during summer vacations and thereby protect their vocations. The cardinals simply refused to accept the U.S. bishops' arguments against villas as contrary to customs of the country and expensive. For the council's agenda, the bishops had to accept villas for major seminaries. The bishops readily accepted other demands of the cardinals: for the major seminary course to in-

---

16. Quoted in White, *Diocesan Seminary,* 151–152.

ACTA ET DECRETA

CONCILII

PLENARII BALTIMORENSIS

TERTII.

A. D. MDCCCLXXXIV.

PRAESIDE

Illmo. ac Revmo. JACOBO GIBBONS,

ARCHIEPISCOPO BALT. ET DELEGATO APOSTOLICO.

BALTIMORAE:

TYPIS JOANNIS MURPHY ET SOCIORUM,

SUMMI PONTIFICIS ATQUE ARCHIEPISCOPO BALTIMORENSIS TYPOGAPHORUM

MDCCCLXXXIV

The Acts and Decrees of the Third Plenary Council of Baltimore that gave direction to the conduct of seminaries in the United States. (Acta et Decreta etc, *Baltimore, 1886)*

clude two years of philosophy and four of theology; faculties in the seminary were to be properly organized especially in regard to philosophy and theology; textbooks were to be used that contained the entire course of theology, lacking nothing but a supplementary explanation from the professor; and qualified instructors were to be appointed. Each ecclesiastical province was to be urged to sponsor a major seminary.[17]

When the U.S. bishops met for their Third Plenary Council of Baltimore in November 1884 at St. Mary's Seminary in Baltimore, they drafted legislation touching on virtually all areas of church life including their most extensive treatment of seminary issues. Consequently, they filled in a great void by providing the canonical blueprint for conducting U.S. diocesan seminaries. Their legislation mandated six years each for major and minor seminary programs. In naming the courses to be taught, the major seminary was to give unprecedented attention to such neglected areas as biblical studies, church history, and homiletics. For the minor seminary, the decree listed the courses in the humanities and sciences for an adequate preparation for the major seminary. As for constructing villas, the bishops simply rejected the idea of confining seminarians in them during the summer. Through this conciliar legislation—though

---

17. "Minutes of Roman Meeting Preparatory to the III Plenary Council of Baltimore I," *The Jurist,* 11 (January 1951), 121–131.

unevenly implemented until the early twentieth century—the seminary is taken from the previous local determination of its needs and standards and is directed to conform to national standards.

In the years following the Third Plenary Council of Baltimore's legislation, the country's diocesan seminaries experienced a burst of creative thought and activity. The conciliar legislation stimulated seminary educators to produce articles and a few books addressing the kind of clerical formation and learning that was necessary for an era of growing challenges to priests from the world of secular learning.[18] In this context, Bishop Bernard McQuaid of Rochester found the laity "demanding more and more of their priests" and "there is less and less room in the ministry for the slow and un-intellectual."[19]

The Catholic institutional landscape likewise changed with the founding of new diocesan seminaries as leading archbishops fulfilled the ideal of each ecclesiastical province sponsoring one. In 1881, the Boston archdiocese had already led the way with the opening of St. John Seminary, Brighton, Massachusetts with a Sulpician faculty. After 1884 several American archbishops adopted the ideal of sponsoring a freestanding seminary with the successful foundings of New York's St. Joseph Seminary (Dunwoodie) at Yonkers, New York (1896); Kenrick Seminary, St. Louis (1894); St. Paul Seminary, Minnesota (1894); and San Francisco's St. Patrick's Seminary at Menlo Park, California (1898). In 1891, the modest diocese of Rochester, New York under Bishop Bernard McQuaid opened St. Bernard Seminary to serve dioceses in its region. Several seminaries were in the forefront of implementing the vision of an improved clerical learning. These seminaries began with adequate funding and were sustained by large enrollments as Catholic immigrant and ethnic communities supplied an ever-growing number of their sons for the priesthood.

Legacy of the Nineteenth-Century Seminary

Through the nineteenth century, the diocesan seminary in the United States made some remarkable transitions from the financially shaky schools of the first half of the century requiring an allied activity such as a lay college to sustain them to the imposing freestanding seminaries at major sees by the century's end. The abbreviated course of studies at early seminaries had given way to a well-developed program of studies at minor and major seminaries emphasizing the needs of ministry in the United States. Through the century church leaders had thereby grappled with issues of the diocesan seminary sometimes by the trial-and-error method. In due course, they dealt with a series of issues: Should each diocese or each ecclesiastical province have a

---

18.   John Talbot Smith, *Our Seminaries: An Essay in Clerical Training* (New York, 1896); John B. Hogan, *Clerical Studies* (Boston, 1898); and occasional articles in *Ecclesiastical Review* (later *American Ecclesiastical Review*), the journal for pastoral theology that began publication in 1889.

19.   Quoted in White, *Diocesan Seminary,* 214.

seminary? Should religious orders and communities of priests sponsor diocesan seminaries? Should the seminary be affiliated with other activities such as lay education? Should priests destined for ministry in the United States be educated abroad? What is the suitable length and content of seminary studies? How could seminaries be funded? Though leaders did not explicitly say so, they were, in effect, experimenting with the formula of the diocesan seminary as first articulated at the Council of Trent and fashioning an American approach. In the process of their experimenting, Roman authority was at first remote, then took the initiative in forming the American College in Rome that seemed to be unwanted, and in ordering the U.S. bishops to hold a plenary council at which they articulated standards for the diocesan seminary in their country.

American responses to the issues related to the diocesan seminary during the nineteenth century stand in marked contrast to what took place in the twentieth century. By then the full consequences of the Ultramontane movement's exalting the papacy had been achieved with Roman authority giving unprecedented direction to the internal life of the Catholic Church. Pope Pius X's condemnation of Modernism in 1907 and the subsequent oath against Modernism cast a dark shadow over theological scholarship and seminary learning for decades. After years of preparation, the Code of Canon Law, issued by Pope Benedict XV in 1917, gave the Catholic Church of the Latin Rite a law code that imposed uniformity of church practices. For the diocesan seminary, the Code prescribed the years of study at six each for minor and major seminary courses, named seminary officials, listed subjects in the curriculum, outlined principles for seminarians' spiritual formation, and made seminary training a condition for ordination. At last the diocesan seminary had a universally applicable canonical blueprint for the training diocesan priests. The Sacred Congregation of Seminaries and Universities, established in 1915, began the regular practice of periodically issuing decrees requiring seminaries to offer new courses in some discipline, to regulate the seminary's internal life, and to raise occasionally the long-standing Roman concern of keeping seminarians in villas during the summer. Trent's principle of the bishop as responsible for directing his seminary was transformed to make him the local agent of Roman authority. The trend of Roman intervention continued through the twentieth century under the Congregation for Catholic Education after Vatican II with more decrees and the famous pontifical visitation of seminaries in the 1980s. In contrast to nineteenth-century practices, the Roman direction of the diocesan seminary in the twentieth century precluded the sustained articulation of an American approach to the diocesan seminary among bishops and seminary educators at least until Vatican Council II. In the nineteenth century, the diocesan seminary along with the other institutions of American Catholic culture represent the great achievements accomplished with limited direction from outside—certainly relatively little from Rome. The nineteenth-century episcopal collegiality and subsidiarity, as foundations of an extraordinary creativity and responsiveness to the needs and opportunities of an immigrant Church in the United States, manifest a now almost forgotten aspect of the authentic Catholic tradition.

"Not the New Woman?":[1] Irish American Women and the Creation of a Usable Past, 1890–1900

Kathleen Sprows Cummings

I n 1896, six Irish-American women addressed the fortieth convention of the Ancient Order of Hibernians (AOH) in Detroit. These women represented the Ladies Auxiliary of the AOH, an organization that had been officially established two years earlier at the Omaha Convention. In Detroit, the Ladies petitioned the board for national recognition and a uniform constitution. The main speaker, Sister Laughlin, emphasized to the national officers of the AOH that she and her colleagues were "not the new women," in spite of their belief in the equality between the sexes.[2] In an article that appeared in the *Catholic World* a year later, Marguerite Moore described the remarkable accomplishment of Mrs. Morrogh-Bernard.[3] According to Moore, Morrogh-Bernard's energetic work in industrial reform had saved the western Irish town of Foxford from destruction. Thanks to her efforts, the formerly depressed village functioned as a thriving mill town. In conclusion, Moore cautiously reminded her readers that the subject of her essay, despite her accomplishments, was quite different from a "new woman."[4] Also in 1897, *Donahue's Magazine* quoted Miss Emma Hemingway in its Women's Deparment. In her valedictory speech at the Woman's College of Baltimore, Hemingway had spoken for her classmates when she declared, "it is not the new woman we emulate, but the true woman."[5]

Who was this new woman, and what compelled Laughlin, Moore, and Hemingway to distinguish themselves from her? The answer to the first question is a simple one. The novelist Henry James had coined the term to describe wealthy women who lived

---

1. "Not the New Woman," *Donahue's Magazine* 38 (1897): 196.
2. Quoted in John O'Dea, *History of the Ancient Order of Hibernians and the Ladies Auxiliary*, vol. III (New York: National Board of the AOH, 1923), 1123.
3. For more information on Agnes Morrogh-Bernard and her activities in Foxford, see Michael Finlan, "Cocking a Snook at Patriarchy to Create an Industrial Marvel," *Irish Times*, 8 May 1992, 12; John Gallagher, *Courageous Irish Women* (Mayo: Fiona Books, 1995), 73–77.
4. Marguerite Moore, "A New Woman's Work in the West of Ireland," *Catholic World* 64 (1897): 458.
5. "Not the New Woman," op. cit.

abroad. He called them "new women" because their fortunes granted them freedom from male control. In the United States, the phrase referred to women who had availed themselves of the new opportunities open to middle-class women in the late nineteenth century. By attending college, earning their own living, working in a settlement house, or otherwise participating in activities outside the home, this new woman challenged the ideology of domesticity of the Victorian era. Financially independent from either a father or a husband, she exercised control over her own life. According to historian Nancy Cott, the new woman "stood for self-development as contrasted to self-sacrifice or submergence within the family."[6] As such, the new woman represents an important transitional figure, a bridge between the "social housekeeper" of the Gilded Age and the early feminists of the Progressive Era.

The answer to the second question—what led the women quoted above to disavow new womanhood—is much more complex. Laughlin, Moore, and Hemingway may have been correct in claiming that they were "not the new women." They were, nevertheless, profoundly influenced by the changing ideas about womanhood that the new woman represented. Like many other Irish-American-Catholic women, they confronted the new possibilities that middle-class America offered them, including a higher degree of participation in what had been exclusively male organizations, more opportunities for leadership roles within the Church and ethnic community, and greater access to institutions of higher education. Ethnicity and religion, however, would shape their response to these opportunities. By rejecting the new woman, Laughlin, Moore, and Hemingway were not resisting these changes. Instead, they were attempting to reconcile tradition with the changing realities of their lives during a time when they and their counterparts were renegotiating what it meant to be Irish, American, Catholic, and female. Laughlin, Moore, and Hemingway's disavowal of new womanhood signaled a broader phenomenon occurring among Irish-American-Catholic women in the 1890s. Creative use of the past helped women establish a necessary distance from the new woman and all she represented; it also, however, allowed them to emulate her in significant ways.

To begin, it is well known that the new woman was always a marginal figure. Almost exclusively white, middle class, and Protestant, she never represented more than a small fraction of American women. Furthermore, it is hardly surprising to find Irish Catholics criticizing new womanhood. After all, the new woman directly challenged the prevailing ideal of Catholic womanhood. Most clearly articulated by Rev. Bernard O'Reilly in *The Mirror of True Womanhood*, this ideology placed the "true woman" in the home, where she might attend to the spiritual and material care of her family. Although she might occasionally leave this sanctuary to perform acts of

---

6. Nancy F. Cott, *The Grounding of Modern Feminism* (New Haven: Yale University Press, 1987), 39. See also Ruth Bordin, *Alice Freeman Palmer: The Evolution of a New Woman* (Ann Arbor: University of Michigan Press, 1993), 2–3.

charity, she could best serve God and the Church by cultivating the faith in her husband and children.[7]

Since the new woman's independence and self-sufficiency challenged this Catholic ideal, she was routinely lambasted throughout the Catholic press. One contributor
to *Donahue's Magazine* urged Catholic women to model themselves on the example
of the Blessed Virgin, rather than follow the "new woman, with all her inconsistencies
and discords."[8]

Given her status as the antithesis of the Catholic "true woman," it is tempting
to conclude that any failure to identify with the new woman indicated conformity
to the prescriptions of a patriarchal Church and an ethnic community characterized
by sharply differentiated gender roles. Indeed, Irish-Catholic failure to resonate with
the new woman or to join her crusades has formed a consistent theme of the historical literature on Irish-American-Catholic women. In *Erin's Daughters in America*, for
example, Hasia R. Diner examined the collective absence of ethnic Irish from the
American woman suffrage movement. She argued that Irish patterns of gender segregation prevented them from participating in what they perceived to be the exclusively
male domain of politics. Diner presented this failure to join the suffrage movement as
a missed opportunity, remarking that Irish-American women, given their myriad of
social problems, would have been "excellent recruits for the feminist struggle to improve the status of women in America and expand their political, economic, and social
vistas." According to Diner, Irish-American women failed to carry an otherwise liber-
ating migration experience to its logical conclusion. Weighed down by "cultural bag-
gage" of the Irish ethnic community, they chose not to join the new woman in seeking
the right to vote.[9]

Other studies of Irish-American women emphasize religion as the primary obstacle
standing between them and the suffrage movement. As members of a Church that con-
sistently defends the traditional concept of womanhood, Catholic women have been
and still remain difficult to situate within a women's history that searches for feminist,
or at least pre-feminist, subjects.[10] Patrick Allit recognized this difficulty in his study

---

7. Rev. Bernard O'Reilly, *The Mirror of True Womanhood* (New York: P. F. Collier, 1877): 6–7. 55–57,
338–39; See also Karen Kennelly, "Ideals of Catholic Womanhood," in *American Catholic Women: A Historical Exploration*, ed. Karen Kennelly (New York: Macmillan, 1989); Penny Edgell Becker, "'Rational
Amusement and Sound Instruction': Constructing the True Woman in the *Ave Maria*, 1865–89," *Religion
and American Culture* 8 (Winter 1998): 55–90.

8. "Occupations for Women," *Donahue's Magazine* 39 (1898): 289.

9. Hasia R. Diner, *Erin's Daughters in America: Irish Immigrant Women in the Nineteenth Century*,
(Baltimore: Johns Hopkins University Press, 1983), 139.

10. Nancy Cott has argued that the term "feminist" cannot be used earlier than 1910. *Grounding of
Modern Feminism*, 13. I have used the term "pre-feminist" as Joseph Mannard does in his article on American Catholic nuns. Mannard borrowed it from Estelle Freedman, "Separatism as Strategy: Female Institution Building and American Feminism, 1870–1930," *Feminist Studies* 5 (Fall 1979): 527, n. 7. Joseph Mannard, "Maternity of the Spirit: Nuns and Domesticity in Antebellum America," *U.S. Catholic Historian* 5
(Fall 1986): 324, n. 38.

of female converts to Catholicism when he observed that because his subjects were "subservient to men, deferential, self-effacing, sometimes anti-suffrage," they "would seem less enticing and least likeable to historians seeking avatars of modern gender role transformations."[11]

On the surface, then, it would seem that denying new womanhood was part and parcel of Irish-American-Catholic women's rejection of the chance to broaden their "political, economic, and social vistas."A closer look, however, suggests that a repudiation of new womanhood did not necessarily imply a resistance to modernity. On the contrary, no matter how ardently they might have denied being new women, the actions of the women quoted above sent quite a different message. The six women who represented the Ladies Auxiliary of the AOH, for example, had taken a very public stance to demand national recognition. Yet, according to Sister Laughlin, she and the other Ladies made no "claim to be speechmakers or political speakers, or anything of that kind."[12] Marguerite Moore, the author of the *Catholic World* feature on Mrs. Morrogh-Bernard, was an Irish American who became a leader in the Irish nationalist movement. Along with Fanny and Anna Parnell, Moore organized an American branch of the Ladies Land League in 1880. In 1920, Moore led British sailors and New York City longshoremen on a three-and-a-half week strike to protest the arrest of two Irish nationalists.[13] Clearly, Moore did not live up to the ideal of the true Catholic woman. For that matter, neither did her heroine, Mrs. Morrogh-Bernard, who had single-handedly revitalized an Irish village. In a similar way, attending college marked a departure from the prescriptions of true womanhood. Yet those who read excerpts of Emma Hemingway's speech in *Donahue's Magazine* were assured that she, too, eschewed new womanhood.

It is difficult to explain this apparent contradiction without situating these women in the context of what was a critical moment in Irish-American Catholic history. By the 1890s, large numbers of ethnic Irish were comfortably situated in the middle-class, and the arrival of hordes of immigrants from Southern and Eastern Europe had effectively nudged them further up the American social, economic, and racial ladder. Although Irish Americans welcomed this change in status, they also worried about what the relative decline in Irish immigration and the fact that many Irish Americans were growing further removed from the immigrant generation meant for the ethnic community as a whole.

Religion further complicated matters. Although finding a place for Catholicism in American life had been a challenge since colonial days, this task took on a new dimension for Irish Americans in the 1890s. For the first time, significant numbers of them had entered the middle class. Just as they had more of a stake in seeking accep-

---

11. Patrick Allit, "American Woman Converts and Catholic Intellectual Life," *U.S. Catholic Historian* 13 (Winter 1995): 79.

12. O'Dea, *History of the AOH*, 122.

13. Joe Doyle, "Striking for Ireland on the New York Docks," in *The New York Irish*, ed. Ronald Baylor and Timothy J. Meagher (Baltimore: Johns Hopkins University Press, 1996), 358.

tance to American society, members of the dominant Protestant culture erected new barriers. The resurgence of anti-Catholic nativism in the 1890s caused the question of what it meant to be both American and Catholic to resound with a renewed sense of urgency. Questions about the compatibility of Catholic faith and American citizenship came from within the Catholic community as well as from the outside. Two distinct factions emerged within the American hierarchy in the late 1880s. One side, the liberals, advocated an assimilationist approach for Catholics and supported measures that would result in a greater degree of Catholic integration into the American mainstream. In contrast to the liberals, conservatives wanted to preserve a distinction between the Catholic Church and American society. They saw the Church as a fortress that would protect Catholics from the evils ingrained in American society.

During a time when Irish American and Catholic were categories under dispute, there was, in theory, little ambiguity about what it meant to be a female member of the community. Catholic gender ideology remained static, as clergy members, advice books, and the Catholic press continued to hold out the "true woman" as the ideal.[14] But the very forces that had propelled the Irish toward the American mainstream made it difficult for women of the community to ignore changes going on around them. Far from being ensconced in an ethnic cocoon, middle-class Irish-American women were aware of and were profoundly influenced by changing ideas about womanhood in American society at large. However, they would respond to them not as new women but as Irish Americans and as Catholics. As Susan Hill Lindley observed in her study of women and religion, women could resist patriarchal prescriptions in one of two ways:

> There are individuals and movements who stepped out of their culturally assigned subordination in society, family or Church; at other times, women appeared to accept subordinate or separate spheres and proceeded to subtly expand their limits.[15]

Becoming new women would have placed Laughlin, Hemingway, and Moore squarely in the former category. Renouncing new womanhood, on the other hand, put them in the latter one. From this position, they could potentially make their new ventures appear not simply legitimate, but even worthy of admiration. Consider, for example, the grounds on which Sister Laughlin denied new womanhood. She claimed to be simply acting as any good Irish woman would, by showing her loyalty to husband, family, Church, and, of course, to Ireland. As Laughlin pointed out, she and her associates had "good, Irish mothers."[16] This qualification established an indisputable boundary between them and the new woman. With this barrier intact, she could legiti-

---

14. Samuel J. Thomas, "Catholic Journalists and the Ideal Woman in Late Victorian America," *International Journal of Women's Studies* 4 (1991): 90.

15. Susan Hill Lindley, *"You Have Stepped Out of Your Place": A History of Women and Religion in America* (Louisville, Ky.: Westminster John Knox Press, 1996), 243–251, 194–195.

16. O'Dea, *History of the AOH*, 1123.

mately deny being a political speaker in the very process of making a political speech. As long as she could convince her audience that she was not a new woman, the irony of this predicament would have escaped both her and her listeners.

Marguerite Moore echoed Laughlin in her explanation of why Mrs. Morrogh-Bernard was not a new woman. First, she had proven her Irish patriotism by rescuing Foxford from decimation; by providing young people with jobs at the mill, she prevented their emigration to America. Second, her work with the Sisters of Charity testified to her piety. Finally, in case loyalty to Ireland and to God were not enough, Moore attributed even more impeccable credentials to her heroine: "Dear readers," she exhorted, "there is no such thing as the new woman; she is just the same one you have known all along since she first sang you to rest."[17] With these words, Moore recast the new woman as "mother."

By defining themselves or their heroines in opposition to the new woman, both Laughlin and Moore transformed women from potential threats into saintly women or mothers. As a result, the prospect of a woman making public speeches or leading industrial reform appeared more palatable to members of a patriarchal Church and an Irish-American society that rigidly demarcated along gender lines. In this manner, they circumvented rather than openly challenged Catholic teaching on womanhood. Laughlin, Moore, and Hemingway were not alone in their effort to present what were essentially new activities as logical continuations of tradition rather than revolutionary departures from it. Throughout the 1890s, many other Irish-Catholic women tried to downplay modern developments by finding Irish or Catholic precedents for them.

As the presence of Sister Laughlin and her cohorts at the AOH convention suggests, new opportunities for women in the Irish nationalist movement opened in the 1890s.[18] Women who joined the movement often creatively used their past to claim that their public work on Ireland's behalf merely continued a long tradition.

Katharine O'Keeffe O'Mahoney, for example, was a teacher from Lawrence, Massachusetts, who was involved in the Irish nationalist movement.[19] She claimed to be following in the footsteps of Margaret O'Carroll, a fifteenth-century Irish woman. Because O'Carroll had successfully defended her hometown of Offaly against invaders, O'Mahoney cited her as justification for a public role for herself and for other women. She wrote that, while the Irish heroine did occasionally leave the shelter of her stately halls, and go forth in a public capacity, it was O'Carroll's "true woman's heart" that inspired these acts. Similarly, O'Mahoney argued that it was her own "true woman's heart" that had inspired, and presumably legitimated, her own public activities on Ireland's behalf.[20]

---

17. Moore, "New Woman's Work," 451, 458.

18. David Brundage, "'In Time of Peace, Prepare for War': Key Themes in the Social Thought of New York's Irish Nationalists," in *New York Irish*, 324.

19 Georgianna Pell Curtis, ed. *American Catholic Who's Who* (St. Louis: B. Herder, 1911), 492.

20. Katharine O'Keeffe O'Mahoney, *Famous Irish Women* (Lawrence: Lawrence Publishing Company, 1907), 59.

Marguerite Moore's feature on Mrs. Morrogh-Bernard represents another area in which Catholic women used the past to broaden their future. Her article was one of many published in Catholic periodicals with the intention of giving more publicity to the charitable work of Catholic women, especially nuns, during the 1890s. This effort was inextricably linked to the Catholic effort to enter the elusive American mainstream. The editors of *Donahue's* Women's Department, for example, argued that Catholic women's natural reticence had obscured their contributions to American society, and as a result, had damaged the "Catholic cause" in the United States. The editors felt this was especially true with regard to women's charitable work. While the public spotlight focused on Protestant women in the settlement house movement, Catholic nuns and lay women served the poor in secret.[21] They sought precedent in the past to demand this greater visibility in American society.

Susan Emery, the editor of the *Sacred Heart Review,* suggested that Catholic women could receive more publicity by coordinating charity work under an umbrella organization that would serve the same purpose for them that the St. Vincent de Paul Society did for men. Characteristically, Emery cited precedent in Catholic history when calling for this innovation; she reported that St. Vincent himself had established a similar organization in 1617.[22]

Of the three disavowals of new womanhood quoted at the beginning of this essay, Hemingway's is perhaps the most representative. The effort to create a usable past was nowhere more prominent than in the arguments in support of higher education for women. During the 1890s, proponents of a Catholic women's college met with particular success in mining the Catholic past for precedent. A contributor to *Donahue's* Women's Department, for example, wondered why the propriety of higher education for women was even the subject of debate, since women's scholarship had been accepted without question throughout most of Catholic history. Of the celebration regarding women's recent achievements in education, this "Chronicler" wrote, "When the history of the elevation of women shall be truly understood, our present tone of exultation may turn into one of regret over time lost since the middle of the sixteenth century."[23] Marie Donegan Walsh echoed this when she wrote about how her visit to Bologna, Italy, convinced her that "there is nothing new under the sun." She marveled at the beauty, femininity, and intellect of the female scholars of the city in ages past. "In an atmosphere of self-congratulation upon Women's colleges and universities," she mused, "can it come as anything but a revelation to find oneself face to face with a city of learned women of long centuries past?"[24]

It was no accident that Catholic periodicals featured so many articles on the subject of women's higher education during the 1890s, the decade in which support for Catholic women's colleges gathered momentum. Although an elaborate system of

---

21. "Suggestions from our Prize Contestants," *Donahue's Magazine* 37 (1897): 182.
22. S. L. Emery, "The Charitable Work of Catholic Women," *Catholic World* 68 (1899): 451.
23. A Chronicler, "Words for Women," *Donahue's Magazine* 34 (September 1895): 1050.
24. Marie Donegan Walsh, "A City of Learned Women," *Catholic World* 75 (1902): 596–97, 598, 608.

higher education for Catholic men was in place by the last decade of the nineteenth century, including the newly established Catholic University of America, no colleges for women existed.[25] Many Catholic girls' academies, since the middle of the nineteenth century, had offered a few outstanding students the opportunity to pursue collegiate instruction through private tutoring.[26] It was not until 1895, however, that the School Sisters of Notre Dame altered the curriculum of their Baltimore academy to incorporate a structured four-year course of study that would result in the conferring of the baccalaureate. The College of Notre Dame of Maryland officially became the first American Catholic women's college when the state legislature awarded them the power to grant the baccalaureate on April 2, 1896.[27] By 1918, fourteen colleges for women appeared on the Catholic Educational Association's approved list of accredited institutions.[28]

Historians have identified several reasons for the development of Catholic women's higher education after 1895. The first was the desire of Catholic women to compete with graduates of secular women's colleges. Irish Catholic women could not help but be affected by the increasing availability of higher education for American women at secular colleges. As the daughters of Irish-Catholic immigrants joined the ranks of the middle class, they needed college degrees to compete with Protestant women for access to white collar occupations. By the end of the century, it was becoming increasingly important for Irish-Catholic women to obtain college degrees, particularly if they wanted to retain their hegemony in the teaching profession.[29] The fear that Catholic women would attend secular institutions prompted widespread concern about the "loss of faith" if they did so. Austin O'Malley, a medical doctor and professor of literature at Notre Dame, believed that Catholic females would succumb even more readily to temptation at these colleges than their male counterparts would.[30]

Events within the Irish-Catholic community provided a second impetus to the development of Catholic women's colleges: the increasing demand for coeducation at men's colleges. The prospect of coeducation posed an even more alarming threat than the possibility of losing the faith. In September 1895, the Catholic University of America began to allow women to attend lectures as "special students." Shortly after that news became public, Bishop John J. Keane, then the rector of the university, declared that the university had no plans to admit women as regular students. Undaunted, twenty women applied to the university in the fall of 1895. Although their

---

25. See Philip Gleason, *Contending with Modernity: Catholic Higher Education in the Twentieth Century* (New York: Oxford University Press, 1995), 3.

26. Sister Mariela Bowler, O.S.F., "A History of Catholic Colleges for Women in the United States of America," (Ph.D. diss.: Catholic University of America, 1933), 19.

27. Sister Mary Cameron, S.S.N.D., *The College of Notre Dame of Maryland, 1895–1945* (New York: Declan X. McMullen Company, Inc., 1947), 56–58.

28. Gleason, *Contending with Modernity*, 70.

29. Ibid., 27.

30. Austin O'Malley, "College Work for Catholic Girls," *Catholic World* 68 (1898): 289–304.

applications were rejected, they indicated the growing demand for higher education among Catholic women.[31]

The fear of women attending secular colleges and the looming threat of coeducation provide logical explanations for the founding of Catholic women's colleges. Neither factor, however, fully explains the complexity behind their development. The founding of institutions of higher learning for Catholic women conveys the compelling example of what happened when Irish-Catholic women confronted the tension between tradition and modernity at the end of the nineteenth century. As such, the founders show how some Irish-Catholic women could be following in the footsteps of the new women while at the same time arguing that they were headed in an opposite direction.

The events surrounding the founding of Trinity College in Washington, D.C., offers an excellent vantage point to view the complexity with which Catholic women encountered and introduced change. Trinity was not the first Catholic women's college, but it was the first to be founded explicitly as a college rather than evolving from a preexisting girls' academy.[32] Trinity was founded by the Sisters of Notre Dame de Namur, an order that had dedicated itself to the education of women. Beginning with the order's founding in Amiens, France, in 1804, the sisters had established elementary schools and teacher training institutes throughout Belgium and England.[33] In 1840, eight Sisters of Notre Dame traveled to the United States to begin teaching the immigrant children of Cincinnati, Ohio. By 1900, the congregation had established twenty-six convents in Ohio, Massachusetts, Pennsylvania, Washington, D.C., and California. In 1897, the sisters had undertaken a new project: the founding of a college for Catholic women in the nation's capital.[34]

Without a doubt, the increasing threat of secular women's colleges provided an incentive for Trinity's founding. Preparing Catholic women to compete with graduates of those institutions was a particular concern of Sister Julia McGroarty, the provincial superior of the Sisters of Notre Dame de Namur. Sister Julia, whose given name was Susan, had been born in Ireland in 1827 and had emigrated to Cincinnati with her family four years later. In 1846, she entered the novitiate of the Sisters of Notre Dame de Namur. She spent the next forty years teaching in their academies in Cincinnati, Roxbury, Massachusetts, and Philadelphia; in 1886, she was appointed the superior of

---

31. Lucy M. Cohen, "Early Efforts to Admit Sisters and Lay Women to the Catholic University of America," in *An Introduction to Pioneering Women at the Catholic University of America*, ed. E. Catherine Dunn and Dorothy A. Mohler (Washington, D.C.: Catholic University Press, 1990); Gleason, *Contending with Modernity*, 28.

32. Mary Oates, C.S.J. "The Development of Catholic Colleges for Women, 1895–1960," *U.S. Catholic Historian* 7 (1988): 414; Mary Hayes, S.N.D. de N, "The Founding of Trinity College, Washington, D.C.: A Case Study in Christian Feminism," *U.S. Catholic Historian* 10 (1991): 84.

33. A Sister of Notre Dame de Namur, *The American Foundations of the Sisters of Notre Dame de Namur* (Philadelphia: Dolphin Press, 1928), x–xvi.

34. Sister Mary Euphrasia, *Sketch of the Foundation*, 1–3.

all of their convents in the United States.[35] As head of Notre Dame's American province, Sister Julia became one of the first American superiors to recognize the need for her students to pursue education beyond the high school level. Accordingly, she redesigned the curriculum to prepare students to study at the college level and opened two Normal Schools to train Catholic women to be teachers.[36] Sister Julia echoed many clergy members when she observed that if Catholics did not provide young women with Catholic institutions, they would "continue to frequent godless schools."[37]

No matter how "godless" they might have seemed, Sister Julia clearly intended to model Trinity on its secular counterparts. Immediately after they began to plan for the college, she and other members of the Notre Dame community studied catalogues of Wellesley and Bryn Mawr to familiarize themselves with their curricula. An early report circulated about the college emphasized that Trinity would be "of the same grade as Vassar, thus giving young women an opportunity for the highest collegiate instruction."[38] During 1899, Sister Julia traveled to Bryn Mawr, Mount Holyoke, Radcliffe, Smith, and Wellesley.[39] These visits forged mutual admiration between secular administrators and the Sisters of Notre Dame that would endure even after Trinity opened. M. Carey Thomas, the president of Bryn Mawr, attended the dedication ceremony in November 1900 to demonstrate support for her "sister college."[40]

As a result of these cooperative efforts, Trinity's curriculum largely resembled that of the secular women's colleges. Trinity offered three four-year courses of study: classical, scientific, and literary. The added requirement of religion explains why Trinity's students needed 132 semester hours to receive a baccalaureate, while most of its secular counterparts maintained a 120–credit requirement.[41] There is much evidence to suggest that the sisters themselves envisioned the founding of Trinity as a decidedly American enterprise. The Ladies Auxiliary Board of Regents,[42] who coordinated fundraising for Trinity, made a conscious decision to appeal to only American sources for aid.[43] The sisters emphasized that the college would be free from foreign control;

---

35. "A Sister of Notre Dame de Namur [Sister Mary Patricia Butler], *An Historical Sketch of Trinity College, Washington, Washington, D.C., 1897–1925,* (Washington, D.C.: n.p., n.d.) 9; Sister Angela Elizabeth Keenan, *Three Against the Wind: The Founding of Trinity College,* (Westminster, Md.: Christian Classics, 1973) 15–29.

36. Annie Toler Hilliard, "An Investigation of Selected Events and Forces that Contributed to the Growth and Development of Trinity College, Washington, D.C. from 1897–1982," (Ph.D. diss.: George Washington University, 1984), 62–64.

37. Sister Julia to Cardinal Rampolla, 8 September 1897, Trinity College Archives, hereafter cited as TCA.

38. M.C.M., "Columbian Reading Union," *Catholic World* 65 (1897): 862.

39. Minutes, LAB, 10 May 1899, TCA; Keenan, *Three Against the Wind,* 124.

40. Lelia Hardin Bugg, "Trinity College," *Rosary Magazine* (April 1901): 377.

41. Sister Columba Mullaly, *Trinity College, Washington D.C. The First Eighty Years, 1897–1977* (Westminster, MD: Christian Classics, 1987), 266.

42. "Trinity College Organizations," pamphlet, "Founding Years," 1897–1901, TCA

43. Minutes of the Ladies Auxiliary Board, 31 March 1898, TCA.

it would fall under the supervision of the provincial superior in Cincinnati rather than the authority of the superior general in Namur, Belgium.[44] Trinity's founding also created some conflict between Sister Julia and her superior at Namur, Mother Aimee. Disagreement over financing the college eventually led Mother Aimee to lose faith in Sister Julia, which she demonstrated by removing California from her jurisdiction in 1901.[45]

Given the affinity between the sisters and the leaders of secular colleges, the similarity in curricula between Trinity and those institutions, and the friction that Trinity's founding generated with Namur, it is not surprising that the college was often heralded as a triumph of the forces of Catholic assimilation. Monsignor Thomas Conaty, Keane's successor as rector of Catholic University, emphasized that the college was of the "utmost importance to Church and state . . . the age demands scholarship, and women's responsibilities urge that intellectual and moral development unite in fitting her to do her full duty to society. . . ."[46]

Another contemporary observer remarked that, because the Catholic girl was "as truly an American girl as any other, of an equally democratic and independent spirit . . . it was not to be expected that there should be any difference in thirst for knowledge."[47] Bishop Thomas Beaven commented that Trinity's founding gave the Sisters of Notre Dame a "distinctly American line" by proving that they were as "in love with country as they were with God."[48] Indeed it seemed that Trinity's founding offered the sisters, their students, and by association, all American Catholics, an opportunity to declare themselves "American."

Clearly, then, Trinity's founding offers an example of how Irish-Catholic women were influenced by changing ideas about womanhood in American society at large. What is intriguing is that the women who founded the college seemed to have quite a different perspective. After their first discussion about the college, Rev. Philip J. Garrigan of Catholic University wrote to the sisters that he hoped "Trinity would do for Catholic women what Bryn Mawr and Vassar had done for American women."[49] The secular influences on the culture notwithstanding, the sisters readily understood Garrigan's distinction. By opening a college for women, they did not believe they were accommodating to American culture; instead, they maintained that they were seeking

---

44. Minutes of LAB, 3 April 1899, TCA. Mary Hayes, S.N.D., argues that the effort to place this distance between the American branch and Namur was deliberate, because Belgium was known for its conservative brand of Catholicism. Hayes, "Founding of Trinity," 81.

45. Sister Joan Bland, S.N.D., "Sister Julia McGroarty," in *Notable American Women, 1607–1950: A Biographical Dictionary*, ed. Edward T. James, et. al. (Cambridge: Belknap Press of Harvard University, 1971), 467.

46. Bugg, "Trinity College," 379.

47. M. McDevitt, "Trinity College and Higher Education," *Catholic World* (June 1904): 389.

48. Most Rev. Thomas Beaven, Bishop of Springfield, to Sister Julia, 14 July 1897, TCA. Excerpts of this were reprinted in a publicity pamphlet.

49. Garrigan to Sister Mary Euphrasia, in *Sketch of the Foundation*, 37.

to "counteract the tendencies of the times."[50] To support this contention, the sisters looked to an Irish and Catholic past.

Like many other Catholic women, Sister Julia saw herself as part of a long and venerable tradition, and she expressed this sentiment in most of her discussions about the college. In Trinity's first catalogue, for example, she expressed her hope that Trinity would "give the women of our day every facility for becoming as brilliant lights as those who have shone in bygone ages—the Hildas, the Liobas, the Marcellas, the Paulas, the Catherines."[51] Sister Mary Euphrasia, the superior of the Notre Dame convent in Washington, D.C., was another founder of the College who believed that modern Catholic women's college students were merely following in the tradition of St. Catherine of Siena and St. Theresa, and the women scholars at Padua. In a letter to Sister Julia, she wrote, "Now the Church approves that we take up the work of Padua!" She pointed out that the Catholic Church had been educating women at Padua three centuries before Harvard, Cornell, or Yale opened their doors to women.[52]

The benefit of establishing a connection to a Catholic past became particularly apparent when the sisters unwittingly became embroiled in the Americanist controversy of the late 1890s. The sisters had anticipated that their proposal to open a college would evoke outrage from traditional opponents of higher education for women, who predicted disaster for the Catholic family and the Church in general should Trinity open. What they had not expected was that the most virulent attacks on the college would come from Catholic prelates and intellectuals who would try to depict the college as another example of Catholic capitulation to American culture. The sisters' alleged alliance with the Americanists nearly prevented them from attaining their goal.

Monsignor Joseph Schroeder, a German-born professor of dogmatic theology at Catholic University, was one of the most forceful opponents of Americanism. He led a faction of German-American Catholics based primarily in the Midwest, and attacked the Americanists through the St. Louis-based paper, *Das Herold des Glaubens* (The Herald of Faith). Schoeder was the nemesis of the liberal Americanists at Catholic University. He had direct access to the pope through his friendship with Cardinal Francesco Satolli, the former apostolic delegate to the United States (who had earlier vetoed proposals to incorporate a women's annex to Catholic University), who had since returned to Rome. Schroeder had used this influence to help engineer the dismissal of Bishop John Keane as rector of Catholic University in September 1896.[53]

Because of its proximity to Catholic University, Trinity became a weapon in the Americanist debate. Clergy on both sides used the college to support their position on

---

50. Sister Mary Euphrasia to Cardinal Satolli, 26 August 1897, TCA.
51. Sister Julia, "Trinity College Catalogue," 1898, TCA.
52. Sister Mary Euphrasia to Sister Julia, 25 May 1897, in *Sketch of the Foundation*, 135–36.
53. Gerald P. Fogarty, S.J., *The Vatican and the American Hierarchy From 1870–1965* (Wilmington, Del.: Michael Glazier, 1985), 158–59; Peter E. Hogan, S.J., *The Catholic University of America, 1896–1903: The Rectorship of Thomas J. Conaty* (Washington, D.C.: The Catholic University of America Press, 1949), 6.

the relationship between Catholicism and American society. Espousing an Americanist position, Cardinal James Gibbons of Baltimore praised Trinity as both a "blessing to our country" and a "glory to our Church."[54] Reverend Edward Pace, a Catholic University professor who would later teach philosophy at Trinity, argued that Catholic women's colleges were needed because the American "democratic spirit" had given Catholic women more potential for achievement.[55]

Monsignor Schroeder, by contrast, saw in Trinity an opportunity to attack indirectly both Americanism and Catholic University. He and his supporters published a series of articles in which they accused the sisters of being "New Women" on the grounds that they were jeopardizing their students' faith and that they were advocating coeducation. In one of the most strident critiques, the editor of *Das Herold des Glaubens* wrote that Trinity's supporters "wanted to imitate Protestants and unbelievers." He argued that they gave little thought to the danger that higher learning would pose to the students' faith. As evidence of what he saw as Trinity's blatant disregard of the Catholic faith, he pointed out that Trinity's admission requirements did not include religion. He claimed, therefore, that Trinity was a non-denominational institution masquerading as a Catholic one, and that the college had only served to strengthen his "old-fashioned conviction that, for the present, man's world should stand at the pinnacle of learning."[56]

Sister Mary Euphrasia responded to this diatribe in a letter to the editors of *Das Herold des Glaubens*, in which she emphasized that Trinity would be no "annex or wing" of Catholic University, and defended the lack of a religion prerequisite by reminding the editors that such a requirement would exclude the very students that Catholic colleges hoped to benefit, those who had attended secular secondary schools.[57] This rejoinder, however, came too late to repair the damage that had already been done. Schroeder and his cohort would likely have been nothing more than a minor annoyance had they not succeeded, with the help of Satolli, in convincing Pope Leo XIII that the sisters were in league with the Americanists. In August 1897, the pope declared that work on Trinity must stop until the matter could be further investigated.[58]

Sister Julia recognized the assault on Trinity as a thinly-veiled attack on the Americanists, and she felt that the charges against the college were unwarranted. She claimed to never have heard of Americanism until she was accused of it.[59] Nevertheless, there was little she or her sisters could do to defend themselves. According to Sister Agnes Loretto, a young nun who accompanied Sister Julia on her travels, the superior's

---

54. James Cardinal Gibbons to Sister Julia, 21 June 1897, TCA.

55. Rev. Edward Pace, Ph.D., "The College Woman," *Donahue's Magazine* 52 (1904): 287.

56. J. N. E., "The 'New Woman' at the 'University'," 11 August 1897, *Das Herold des Glaubens*, translation in "Founding Years," TCA. Evidence that Schroeder was behind this letter can be found in a letter from Sister Angela Elizabeth S.N.D., to Sister Sheila Doherty, 2 June 1972, TCA. "J. N. E." is most likely John N. Enzelberger, a German priest from Illinois and the editor of *Das Herold des Glaubens*.

57. Sister Mary Euphrasia to Editors of *Das Herold des Glaubens*, 28 August 1897, TCA.

58. SME, *Sketch of the Foundation*, 195.

59. Keenan, *Three Against the Wind*, 112.

frustration increased as the summer waned. She confided to Sister Agnes that "if she was a man, she could put on her hat and go off to see the pope."[60] Unable to "go off to see the pope," as she wished, Sister Julia and Sister Mary Euphrasia pleaded Trinity's case through a letter-writing campaign. Because they had learned that Cardinal Satolli was "hand in glove" with Monsignor Schroeder, they addressed their letters to Cardinal Dominic Ferrata, the cardinal protector of the Sisters of Notre Dame de Namur, and Cardinal Mariano Rampolla, the Secretary of State.[61]

In these letters, the sisters tried to make several points. First, they insisted that they were not imitating secular schools but providing a Catholic alternative to them. Sister Julia reminded Cardinal Rampolla that in the United States, education was the "cry of the age."[62] Sister Mary Euphrasia dramatized the disaster by providing proof of what would happen if Catholic women continued to enroll in non-Catholic institutions; she reported that at Colombian University (later George Washington University), a Baptist University in D.C., eleven Catholic students had "lost the faith" over a four-year period.[63] Also, they attempted to correct the erroneous reports about coeducation. Sister Julia attributed these rumors to "the spirit of opposition in the Western Churches."[64] In another letter, she wrote that "anyone who knows the order [Notre Dame] will recognize [the rumors about coeducation] as gratuitous."[65]

Although the sisters used these two common arguments—the competition from secular schools and the threat of coeducation—to support their cause, they also emphasized Trinity's connection to the past. They reminded the bishops that religious teaching had long been the "alpha and omega" of Notre Dame's philosophy of education.[66] In a letter to Cardinal Rampolla, Sister Julia wrote, "With the memory of Italy's renown in its women saints and scholars as the law and guide of Trinity College, we pray for our work."[67]

Good news arrived in late October, when the apostolic delegate announced that the Holy See would no longer interfere with the sisters' plans. Conaty advised the sisters not to gloat over their victory: "Do not exult too loud, but proceed joyfully in secret, grateful that the difficulty has been overcome."[68] The sisters allowed themselves to rejoice privately, however: "Glory be to God in all things! We can build our college as soon as we have money enough, and go right on without minding what anyone says to us," wrote Sister Agnes Loretto enthusiastically.[69]

---

60. Sister Agnes Loretto to Sister Superior [Sister Mary Borgia], 15 September 1897, TCA.

61. Sister Helen Louise, S.N.D., *Sister Julia [Susan McGroarty]* (New York: Benziger Brothers, 1928), 273; SME, *Sketch of the Foundation*, 230.

62. Sister Julia to Cardinal Rampolla, 8 September 1897, TCA.

63. Sister Mary Euphrasia to Cardinal Satolli, 26 August 1897, TCA.

64. Sister Julia to Cardinal Ferrata, 8 September 1897, TCA.

65. Sister Julia to Cardinal Alois Maselli, September 1897, TCA.

66. Sister Mary Euphrasia to Cardinal Satolli, 26 August 1897, TCA.

67. Sister Julia to Cardinal Rampolla, 8 September 1897, TCA.

68. Quoted in A Sister of Notre Dame [Sister Mary Patricia Butler], *An Historical Sketch,* 15.

69. Sister Agnes Loretto to Sister Superior [Sister Mary Borgia], 26 October 1897, TCA.

That the founding of Trinity became so intertwined with the Americanist controversy demonstrates how easily gender could be manipulated to serve other purposes. Members on both sides of the debate used gender to either impugn or defend the Americanist position. Supporters exalted them as true women; opponents assailed them as new women. Luckily for Trinity, its supporters triumphed; by October 1897, Schroeder had been discredited by his enemies at Catholic University and would leave there by the end of the year.[70] Although it was Schroeder's rapidly declining influence—and not the sisters' letter-writing campaign—that was the most significant factor in Rome's decision to permit the sisters to continue, the whole episode does suggest that finding links to the past could at times be strategic. Establishing a connection to Padua lent credence to the sisters' arguments that Trinity was different from its secular counterparts. It provided, therefore, an important defense against the accusation that they were behaving like new women.

The frequency with which the sisters and their supporters celebrated Trinity's links to the past suggests, however, that their doing so was more than just a matter of expediency. Even after the crisis had passed, Trinity's advocates continued to distinguish its students from the ubiquitous new woman:

> While the New Woman, with her head full of vagaries, is reconstructing the Universe, Trinity College will offer to her Catholic sisters an opportunity to accrue knowledge which, through adapting itself to all rightful demands of the period, is firmly wedded to that unchanging faith which has lifted woman in all ages to her true position.[71]

Trinity's first students were told that they were ". . . reviving an old privilege conferred by the Church on women centuries before the discoverer of America was born, the privilege of being learned and good." To underscore this connection to their Catholic past, statues of "St. Paula, St. Katherine, Laura Bassi, wearing the cap and gown of the University of Bologna, Helena Bisopiagia, the sunny-haired Venetian, first among the philosophers of her time, and Novella d'Andrea" greeted students when they walked on the terrace of Trinity's main building.[72]

Catholic women's celebration of the past instead of progress strikes an incongruous note in an era defined by transformations in all areas of American life, and in particular in gender roles. Stepping outside the boundaries of Catholic true womanhood, however, could place women in a very precarious situation; looking backward helped protect them from this vulnerability. Blending tradition and innovation made sense to

---

70. In what Archbishop John Ireland dubbed the "War of 1897," the Americanist contingent at Catholic University launched an offensive against Schroeder, and collected witnesses who testified that he had been out all night imbibing at disreputable saloons. In October 1897, they presented this evidence to the Vatican, and the University's Board of Trustees voted for dismissal. At the request of the Pope, Schroeder was permitted to resign, which he did on December 29, 1897. He departed Catholic University defeated and disgraced. Gleason, *Contending with Modernity*, 10; Fogarty, *Vatican and the American Hierarchy*, 158–59.

71. Mary T. Waggaman, "Catholic Life in Washington," *Catholic World* 66 (March 1898): 837–38.

72. Bugg, "Trinity College," 388.

them as Irish American Catholics in a way that becoming new women did not. By appropriating an Irish and Catholic past, women like Laughlin, Moore, Hemingway, and Sister Julia embraced change on their own terms, and in the process carved out a future for themselves that allowed them more opportunities and more choices. These Irish American women show how and why women could both forswear new womanhood and redefine the parameters of the female experience; their story, therefore, illustrates that becoming new women was not the only path to modernity for women during the Progressive era.

The Power of Ethnicity in a Community of Women Religious: The Poor Handmaids of Jesus Christ in the United States, 1868–1930

Anita Specht

On August 15, 1868, Mother Mary Katherine Kasper (1820–1898), the foundress of the Poor Handmaids of Jesus Christ, conducted eight sisters from their motherhouse in Dernbach, Germany, to the docks at Le Harve, France, where they would embark for the United States. She had been asked by Bishop John Henry Luers of the Fort Wayne Diocese in Indiana to send sisters to serve in a German immigrant parish there. Upon careful consideration, she designated Mary Rosa Blum (the first superior of the American province), Mary Eudoxia Bender, Mary Hyacintha Neuroth, Mary Matrona Möring, Mary Facunda Wand, Mary Bella Sieroecke, Mary Henrica Sieroecke, and Mary Corona Jahn to make the journey. After receiving special blessings from three priests who accompanied them to the steamship, the sisters tearfully boarded the boat singing the Marian hymn "Direct Our Boat Through the Waves, O Mother." As it slipped out of the harbor, Mother Kasper wrote: "At last, I too, could weep and my eyes followed the boat as long as possible."[1] When the sisters arrived in Hesse Cassel, Indiana, on August 30, they began a new chapter in the history of the Poor Handmaids of Jesus Christ.

For the Poor Handmaids, the maintenance of ethnicity held tangible benefits. Their communal bonds in the United States were strengthened by connections to Germany that were both symbolic and administrative. In addition, the sisters gained entry into American parishes in the Midwest because they could serve the German immigrants who lived in them. They also used their association with German Americans to fund their projects. This does not mean that islands of Germanness were maintained in a sea of American Catholicism. The order faced several crises over Americanization, but by 1930 the sisters accommodated those aspects of the American environment which

---

1. Mother Kasper to the Poor Handmaids of Jesus Christ (P.H.J.C.) community, August 15, 1868. File CHJC 1/7, Archives of the University of Notre Dame (hereafter abbreviated AUND).

could assure the survival of their community and at the same time retained a link to the motherhouse in Dernbach, Germany.

This contrasts sharply with many historical studies of women religious which concentrate on the transformation of European orders into "American" ones, detailing ethnic conflict, rule changes, and ultimately the separation of American convents from their European motherhouses. Mainly, these analyses contend that, to succeed as an American religious community, an order needed to adopt English, abolish class distinctions among the nuns, and recruit candidates from various ethnic backgrounds. The Poor Handmaids in America did not follow this pattern. They attracted members from the German-Catholic parishes they served, had no class distinctions, adopted English fairly quickly, and kept strong ties with Europe.[2]

The order originated as part of the Catholic devotional revolution of the nineteenth century. As the church formalized clerical education, classified acceptable devotions, and tried to regulate pilgrimage sites, it reclaimed the public presence it had lost when European governments secularized church properties, and it opposed aspects of modernity that seemed to threaten the viability of its institutions, such as republicanism, communism, and the exploitation of labor. For many ordinary Catholics, the devotional revolution gave them an opportunity to participate in mass pilgrimages or to see the church as the means to heal social ills.[3]

Katherine Kasper drew strength and inspiration from this Catholic revival. She grew up in a peasant family of seven children in Dernbach and lived in a region called the Westerwald, the most impoverished part of the Duchy of Nassau in Germany. As a child, Katherine was pious and especially liked to reflect upon the virtue of poverty. She also spent time at the local shrine, the Heilborn, praying to the Virgin Mary. Like all farm girls at this time, she worked in the stable, fields, and forest. Because her family needed her labor, she only managed to attend school for approximately two years. When her father, Henry, died, she supported her mother, also named Katherine, by hiring out as a farm hand and household servant in neighboring towns. She also worked in her own community hauling wood, shoveling snow, and maintaining the roads that ran past her father's property. One day, as she worked with the local road crew, she received a vision in which she marched at the head of a proces-

2. Margaret Susan Thompson, "Sisterhood and Power: Class, Culture, and Ethnicity in the American Convent," *Colby Library Quarterly* 25 (September 1989): 149–175. Margaret Susan Thompson, "Cultural Conundrum: Sisters, Ethnicity, and the Adaptation of American Catholicism," *Mid-America* 74 (October 1992): 205–230. Carol K. Coburn and Martha Smith, *Spirited Lives: How Nuns Shaped Catholic Culture and American Life, 1836–1920* (Chapel Hill: University of North Carolina Press, 1999), 41–66.

3. Emmet Larkin, "The Devotional Revolution in Ireland, 1850–1878," *American Historical Review* 77 (1972): 627–652. David Blackbourn, *Marpingen: Apparitions of the Virgin Mary in Nineteenth-Century Germany* (New York: Alfred A. Knopf, 1994). Wolfgang Schieder, "Church and Revolution: Aspects of the Social History of the Trier Pilgrimage of 1844," in *Conflict and Stability in Europe*, ed. Clive Emsley (London: Croom and Helm, 1979), 65–95. Ruth Harris, *Lourdes: Body and Spirit in the Secular Age* (New York: Viking, 1999).

*Mother Mary Katherine Kasper
(1820–1898)
(All photos in this article are courtesy:
Archives of the University of Notre Dame)*

sion of women religious dressed in the habit that would eventually identify the Poor Handmaids.

Driven by a desire to help people in misery, Katherine felt called by God to help the sick and began to tend patients free of charge in 1842. While she took care of her elderly mother, she still continued her nursing and gathered several women to take care of the household. These women later voluntarily helped her nurse the sick, and together they formed a *Mädchenverein,* or young women's society. Under the direction of the local priest, Father Josef Heimann, the group began a routine of regular confession and communion and received guidance on living in community. In 1846, this group formed an association of charity and Katherine submitted its statutes to her priest. The society dedicated itself to the Virgin Mary and pledged to follow the virtues of humility, chastity, and poverty while serving their neighbors by nursing the sick. Five years later, Peter Joseph Blum, bishop of Limburg, approved the transition of the group from a lay women's society to a religious order and authorized the constitution of the Poor Handmaids of Jesus Christ; he also administered the vows on the Feast of of Mary's Assumption, August 15, 1846. The constitution of the order, modeled on that of the Sisters of Charity, grounded the community in Canon Law. Since the Sisters of Charity were historically related to the Daughters of Charity of Vincent de Paul and Louise de Marillac, particularly through their common ministries, the Poor Handmaids of Jesus Christ also specified their commitments to the teaching and nursing ministries when they professed their traditional vows of poverty, chastity and obedience.

The rules also provided a system of governance led by an elected mother general who was advised by a council and whose regional divisions were administered by provincial superiors. By 1880, the total number of sisters had risen to 688, and 1898, the year of Mother Kasper's death, the order had 1,725 members.[4]

Mother Kasper wanted to show a way for sisters to achieve spiritual perfection by following the order's rule, and this rule became the glue which bound the German and American sections of the community together. "Let us comply truly and publicly to our instructions and rules," Sister Mary Hyacintha Neuroth wrote to the sisters in America, "then we will be happy in vocation and in the community. Let us support the rule, and the rule will support us."[5] A German immigrant, Sister Hyacintha was the provincial superior of the Poor Handmaids in the United States from 1895–1904. The rule was translated into English in December 1910 after the Mother General Mary Amalia heard that the American sisters wanted to read the rules in their "mother tongue." She reminded them to "always read these constitutions with great reverence; God our Lord speaks to you through them."[6] As the sisters on both sides of the Atlantic adhered to the same constitution, the American sisters retained an important ethnic connection to Germany.

This connection was further strengthened as both groups participated in the same rituals and drew inspiration from each other. During a retreat in Germany, Mother Kasper extolled the self-sacrificing work of the Poor Handmaids who worked in the Chicago smallpox hospital during an epidemic.[7] The American sisters provided an important example of a mortified life to the whole order. They also earned praise from the Chicago newspapers for their service, garnering public notice for Catholicism which could counter the negative stereotypes that flourished in both Germany and the United States. When Mother Kasper died in 1898, all of the sisters mourned her loss, and Sister Hyacintha ordered each mission in America to offer two masses for the repose of her soul. In addition, each sister was to offer three holy communions, recite the way of the cross for nine days, as well as saying the rosary, the De Profundis, the

---

4. Reverend George T. Meagher, C.S.C., *With Attentive Ear and Courageous Heart: A Biography of Mother Mary Kasper, Foundress of the Poor Handmaids of Jesus Christ* (Milwaukee: Bruce Press, 1957), 8–43. Walter Bröckers, "Maria Katharina Kasper (1820–1898)," in *Die Neuen Heiligen: Große Christen auf dem Weg zur Heilig- oder Seligsprechung,* ed. Günther Beugrand (Augsburg: Pattloch Verlag, 1991), 188–190. February 5, 1855, Letter to the Ducal Ruling Authority of the Land of Nassau in Wiesbaden from Katharina Kasper in file CHJC 1/05 AUND.

5. Sister M. Hyacintha Neuroth, provincial superior of the American province, to the sisters in America, December 1900. Located in the file titled "Provincial Circular Letters: Sister Hyacintha (original transcripts) 1897–1908," CHJC 15/10, AUND. In the German language document, the word "Genossenschaft" was used which I have interpreted as "community." A literal translation would be "cooperative society" or "partnership."

6. *Constitutions of the Congregation of the Poor Handmaids of Jesus Christ at Dernbach* (Freiburg: B. Herder, 1911), frontispiece. Located in the file "Constitutions of the Congregation of the Poor Handmaids of Jesus Christ," CHJC 100/11, AUND.

7. Fourth conference given by Mother Mary Katherine Kasper, April 17, 1894. Located in file "Conferences Given by Mother Mary, English Translations, 1894–1895," CHJC 1/28, AUND.

The fourteen holy helpers' altar located in the chapel in the woods.

Our Father, and reciting the litany for the dead for four weeks.[8] This served to remind the Americans of the connection to their German origins and brought them together with their German counterparts in mourning the death of the foundress. In the 1930s, after the congregation moved to a new motherhouse in Donaldson, Indiana, the sisters built what they called "the chapel in the woods." It looked similar to the Heilborn shrine which had been so important to Mother Kasper, and inside they erected a display of the fourteen holy helpers. The devotion to the fourteen holy helpers was most popular in Germany, Poland, and Czechoslovakia. This is an example of the way the American sisters tried to create the cultural elements that could reinforce commonalities between both segments of the Poor Handmaids.

Another way to maintain common outlooks and practices within the group was to ensure that the administrative ties between Germany and the United States remained strong. From 1868 until 1932, the superiors of the American province came from Germany and were women experienced in the organizational life of the community. In addition to the superiors, the mother general sent sisters from Germany to the United

---

8. Sister Mary Hyacintha to the sisters of the American province, February 2, 1898. Located in file "Correspondence between Dernbach and Fort Wayne, 1880–1909," CHJC 5/19, AUND.

States on several occasions, most of whom remained there. In the summer of 1898, the first representative of the mother general visited America. Similarly, groups of American sisters visited the motherhouse in Germany, usually to attend the general chapter meetings.[9]

More frequently than personal visits, letters went back and forth across the Atlantic. Several times a year, the mother general sent a letter to the whole community that stressed communal solidarity based on the rule. As Mother Kasper told the sisters in America: "If you strive to keep the holy rule, if you are zealous in practicing virtue, you are closer to the congregation and to me than a sister who lives a mediocre life even though she may live in the motherhouse."[10] Supplementing these circular letters, the superiors in America corresponded with Germany on administrative matters, big and small. Superiors in the United States wrote for advice on transfers, the minimum age for novices, and expansions. Letters were also exchanged regarding the color of aprons and the inappropriate use of prayers before and after sisters renewed their vows.[11] The visits, letters, and concerns about the seemingly mundane matter of aprons kept them united in daily habits. Even though an ocean separated northern Indiana from western Germany, both sections of the order operated under the same assumptions about the elements that defined them as Poor Handmaids.

Those assumptions were maintained because the women who joined in the United States came from German or German-American backgrounds. From 1868–1930, the community experienced steady growth. During this period, a total of 1,109 women entered as postulants. Their average age was 21 with a median age of 20.[12] The percentage of foreign born averaged 34 percent with this percentage dropping steadily after 1900 when German immigration to the United States slowed. Almost all of the foreign-born postulants came from Germany or from areas of eastern Europe colonized by German speakers such as Poland or the territories of Austria-Hungary. Of the 989 women who stayed through the novitiate and professed their first vows, 667 or 67 percent had at least one foreign-born parent from Germany or the Germanic regions. Only six of the 989 came from families originating in Ireland, a country which supplied the bulk of candidates to most religious orders in the United States.[13] These

---

9. File "Ancilla Domini Chronicle, 1918–1926," translated by Sister M. Antonita Altmix, CHJC 33/4, UNDA, pages 24–25. File "Ancilla Domini Chronicles in German, 1893–1927," CHJC 33/2, AUND, pages 20 and 174.

10. Mother Kasper to the American sisters, September 3, 1884. Located in the file "Selected Collection of the Most Beautiful Letters of Mother Mary Katherine Kasper to Her Spiritual Daughters, PHJC (English), 1867–1898," CHJC 1/21, AUND.

11. Letters from Sr. M. Ligouria to Sr. M. Hyacintha, superior of the American province, December 4, 1897, July 7, 1897, November 27, 1896, April 13, 1896. Located in file "Correspondence of Sr. M. Ligouria, 1896–1908," CHJC 5/16, AUND.

12. File "Register of Sisters—Entrance Book I, 1869–1916," CHJC 18/01, AUND and file "Entrance Book II," CHJC 18/02, AUND. The median age is a more accurate representation of the age of the women who entered the Poor Handmaids because it factors out ages that are unusually high or low.

13. File "Register of Sisters," CHJC Box 95, AUND.

hereditary ties with Germany provided a common set of experiences and idioms that could help the German and American communities understand each other.

Aside from the religious and cultural ties that enhanced the sisters' ethnic identity, the community had powerful social incentives to associate with their German heritage. They used their links with Germany to gain a foothold in German-American parishes like St. Boniface in Germantown, Illinois, or to build hospitals and convents where pockets of German immigrants settled like New Ulm, Minnesota, or the old northwest side neighborhood of Chicago. In several cases, they were able to more easily win the support of bishops and priests because of their national origins. Bishop John Henry Luers of Fort Wayne, Indiana, who immigrated as a child from Münster, Westphalia, Germany, requested the sisters' services in the United States and helped them establish their first hospital there in 1869. In 1908, Father Louis A. Moench, originally of Freudenberg, Baden, Germany, arranged to have the sisters own and operate a Catholic hospital in Mishawaka, Indiana, because they had served the German Americans in his parish of St. Joseph's, and he knew of their strong reputation as nurses and hospital administrators. In 1886, Archbishop Patrick Feehan of Chicago requested that the Poor Handmaids build "*eines Deutschen Krankenhauses*" or a "German hospital" in the city. This petition culminated in the construction of St. Elizabeth's Hospital on the corner of LeMoyne and Claremont.[14] In each case, the sisters' ethnicity helped them gain an entrée into the church's power structure that would enable them to perform service to the sick and poor, as their rule mandated.

Their ethnic connections also helped them gain the support of the immigrant community for funds and other support for schools and hospitals. To establish St. Joseph's Hospital in Fort Wayne, Bishop Luers incorporated the St. Joseph's Benevolent Association on April 22, 1869. Financing for the project came when the association sold stock for $25.00 per share which people in Fort Wayne and the surrounding countryside purchased. Of the people who bought them, at least 76 percent had recognizably German surnames, which indicates that the overwhelming base of support for the hospital came from the German Americans near Fort Wayne. Similarly, when Mishawaka set out to raise $10,000 to build the new St. Joseph's Hospital, families with the German surnames Herzog, Gerstbauer, Schellinger, and Konzen funded hospital rooms while Joseph Ganser contributed a large statue of St. Joseph.[15] Just as important as the support of German Americans was the financial support of the motherhouse in Germany. When the American provincial superior, Sister Mary Secunda Germersheimer,

---

14. Sr. Mary Aletha, "Rockhill's Folly Site Now St. Joseph's Hospital," *The News Sentinel* (Ft. Wayne, Indiana), May 1926. Located in the file "St. Joseph's Hospital—History of, Early Days," CHJC 68/26, UNDA. *A Century of Catholic Faith in Mishawaka, 1848–1948*, page 40. Located in file "St. Joseph's Hospital Souvenir Books," CHJC 73/26, AUND. File "St. Elizabeth's Hospital Chronicles, 1887–1912," CHJC 47/3, UNDA.

15. Files "Ft. Wayne—St. Joseph's Hospital—Capital Stock Certificate Book, 1869–1875," CHJC 69/2, UNDA and "St. Joseph Hospital Chronicles, 1910–1951," CHJC 73/1, AUND and "Mishawaka, IN—St. Joseph Hospital—Annual Reports, 1912–1926," CHJC 111/07, AUND.

presented the idea for St. Elizabeth's Hospital to Mother Kasper in Dernbach, she received an assurance of financial support from the German motherhouse, which culminated in a loan of $4,815.[16] The sisters maintained a web of connections based on their ethnic identity. They were valuable to the Catholic church in America because they could serve German Americans, and they drew considerable financial support from that ethnic base.

When the order established new missions, ethnicity played a decisive role. The sisters wanted to stay in areas settled by people who held cultural views similar to their own. At the same time, they had to adapt to conditions in America that they had not faced in Europe. When invited to a neighboring farm for supper, they found clouds of flies swarming around the table and could hardly keep from laughing when they saw the farmer's daughter swishing the flies away with a leafy branch while the adults ate. They learned how to climb over fences while wearing a long black habit. They tried to cook pumpkins but ended up with a small, solid pan of pumpkin mush which they mixed with milk and ate for lunch because they were hungry and could not afford other food.[17]

The group also adapted to the American environment as they gradually incorporated English into the life of the community. The first pioneer sisters began to learn English immediately.[18] By the 1890s, the sisters' retreats included both German and English elements.[19] However, this did not prevent one sister from leaving because she could not understand the German language. Sister Mary Symplicia, born Ludowika Monka in Goray Farnikan, West Prussia, left the order on August 12, 1899, after three years of vowed religious life. The chronicle stated that "she entered a community from her own nation," probably an order associated with her ethnic group in West Prussia.[20] In 1911, at a provincial meeting, the Poor Handmaids in America decided to use English to record their corporate affairs and elections while retaining German for private documents and entrance records.[21] From 1868 to 1930, most of the chronicles were kept in German, and even as late as 1961, notations of deaths were made in neat, nineteenth-century German handwriting in the entrance books. Language was used in a practical way. If it facilitated the spiritual progress of a sister to conduct retreats in English or to translate the rules, that transition was viewed in a positive light. The sisters never allowed language differences to be a divisive factor in their group. Their first priority was to diligently follow the rule, and they could do this in both Germany and the United States, speaking English or German.

---

16. File "St. Elizabeth's Hospital Chronicles, 1887–1912," CHJC 47/3, AUND.

17. File "German Chronicle—Poor Handmaids of Jesus Christ in America," CHJC 113/16, AUND.

18. File "German Chronicle—Poor Handmaids of Jesus Christ in America," CHJC 113/16, AUND.

19. File "Ancilla Domini Chronicles in German, 1893–1927," CHJC 33/2, AUND, pages 4, 33, 77, 83, 86, 91, 93, 103.

20. File "Ancilla Domini Chronicles in German, 1893–1927," CHJC 33/2, AUND, page 55.

21. *Articles of the Community of the Poor Handmaids of Jesus Christ*, page 2. Located in file "Annual and Special Meetings of the Poor Handmaids of Jesus Christ," CHJC 7/10, AUND.

However, at several points in their early history in the United States, the Poor Handmaids had to make decisions about how far to adapt to the American environment and whether to maintain the ties to Germany. The first of these crisis points occurred in 1885 and the second during World War I. The 1885 incident began on April 30, 1885, when the provincial superior, Sister Mary Prudentia, left for Germany and was replaced on July 18 by Sister Mary Secunda who arrived from Europe. To justify her decision, Mother Kasper explained that Sister Prudentia had served for thirteen years as a provincial superior, even though the rule stipulated that nine years was the maximum tenure allowed in such a post. Mother Kasper reassured those in the American province, writing "you are receiving another good provincial. English conditions, culture and manners are not foreign to her."[22] Unfortunately, Sister Prudentia did not want to leave the United States, and her reluctance stirred up a controversy among the sisters in Fort Wayne and in the diocesan hierarchy. It originated with issues of ethnic identity. Some felt that Sister Prudentia made too many concessions to the American environment and would sever connections with the motherhouse in Dernbach.

The situation culminated on September 14, 1885, when a group of sisters at St. Joseph's Hospital in Fort Wayne wrote to Mother Kasper. Supporting her decision to replace Sister Prudentia, they asserted that, if Sister Prudentia were allowed to return to America, "it [would] mean the separation from the German motherhouse."[23] The women who wrote the letter, Sister Mary Athanasia and an unnamed group of "sisters who wish well for the congregation," identified themselves with a group of older sisters who would have returned to Europe on the next boat if Sister Prudentia had come back to the United States. In contrast, the "younger sisters" would have agreed to form a separate congregation. The letter only hinted at Sister Prudentia's shortcomings, saying that she had given "sins and offences to God" through her conduct and inspired feelings of bitterness that caused her to lose the love and respect of the sisters who wrote the letter.[24] This was an important event in the Poor Handmaids' history in the United States. It indicates that a substantial group of the sisters were committed to Mother Kasper and to the rule she instituted for the order in spite of pressures to break from Germany and start a new American order. It also shows the importance of a strong administrative system. Mother Kasper replaced a superior of questionable loyalty with one committed to an order based in Germany. At the same time, the new superior, Sister Secunda, was chosen because she could adapt to American customs. The leaders of the community clearly believed that obedience to the rule would not necessarily be compromised if the sisters adapted to the new country, unless those adaptations caused them to reject the rule entirely.

---

22. Letter from Mother Kasper to the American province, June 24, 1885. Located in file "Correspondence of Mother Mary Katherine Kasper (English) 1882–1885," CHJC 1/14, AUND.

23. Letter from Sr. M. Athanasia, and all sisters who wish well for the congregation, to Mother Kasper, September 14, 1885. Located in file "Correspondence Regarding the Transfer of the Provincial Superior," CHJC 1/16, AUND.

24. Ibid.

The second ethnic crisis for the order occurred with the outbreak of World War I. "On Good Friday, the 6th of April," the chronicler for the motherhouse recorded in 1917, "was learned the dreadful report that America, our [dear] fatherland, had declared war against Germany, upon which we were all deeply shocked."[25] The war forced many German Americans to renounce their ties to Germany and adopt the mantle of one-hundred percent Americanism. Many changed their names, refused to speak German, and abandoned their ethnic clubs and activities.[26] Even though the sisters considered America their homeland, they understood that their German background placed them in a vulnerable position. During the summer of 1918, while Sister Mary Gonzaga Knaack tried to study for a doctorate in education at Catholic University of America, government officials forced her to leave Washington, D.C. They apparently felt she was a spy or a subversive, despite her more than twenty-eight year residency in the United States.[27] German-born sisters in Fort Wayne and Chicago had to register with local officials. Those in Fort Wayne signed three documents testifying to their status, had their pictures taken, and were fingerprinted like common criminals.[28]

Wartime restrictions also interfered with important functions of the community. In 1918, Mother Tabitha Swickert, a German citizen and the provincial superior, was advised not to visit the retreat held at the Germantown, Illinois, convent for fear she might be attacked.[29] To protect their assets from possible seizure, the Poor Handmaids changed their corporate officers. On July 12, 1918, the sisters assembled for their annual meeting and elected Sister Mary Catherina as the corporation president, replacing Mother Tabitha. Next, they elected Sister Mary Lydia Kroeger vice-president, Sister Mary Symphorosa Louen secretary, and Sister Mary Matrona Weber treasurer, all American citizens.[30]

The war accelerated the sisters' outward identification with American institutions. Several of them took American citizenship, including Sister Gonzaga who became a citizen in June 1921. Most notably, Mother Tabitha received American citizenship on February 28, 1925, along with two other sisters, Sister Mary Adelrika and Sister Mary Germana Gramling. When she did this, the chronicle recorded, she became the first American provincial superior of the Poor Handmaids. In 1921, some registered to vote in local elections. Assessing the process, the chronicler wrote: "This is no pleasant thing but nowadays one must take part in it."[31]

The First World War made the Poor Handmaids conscious of their role as citizens. This received its concrete expression in May 1925 when workmen dug a ten foot-deep

25. File "Ancilla Domini Chronicles in German, 1893–1927," CHJC 33/2, AUND, page 200.

26. Frederick C. Luebke, *Bonds of Loyalty: German Americans and World War I* (DeKalb, Ill.: Northern Illinois University Press, 1974).

27. File "Ancilla Domini Chronicles in German, 1893–1927," CHJC 33/2 AUND, pages 217, 227.

28. Ibid., 216.

29. Ibid.

30. Ibid., 218.

31. Ibid., 255, 258.

foundation to support an eighty-six foot flagpole. It took twelve men to set it. On Memorial Day, the sisters raised an American flag, sang patriotic songs, and lowered the flag to half mast in memory of fallen soldiers. "This way," the chronicle recorded, "the public sees that we are also Americans."[32] World War I forced German Americans to exhibit their citizenship in public ways. The Poor Handmaids responded to this pressure in ways that fulfilled the requirements of citizenship, but they also were concerned that citizenship might exact a toll on their community life. By engaging in the public rituals of American citizenship, they could drift from the principles set for the order by Mother Kasper in the nineteenth century.

The community revitalized the links with its origins and with the sisters in Germany when Mother General Mary Firmata visited the United States province from January to July 1924. During her stay, Mother Firmata visited all of the convents, even making special arrangements to stop in tiny Arcola, Indiana. She received masses in her honor, bouquets of flowers, and a new pair of eye glasses from an optometrist in Fort Wayne. Before she returned to Germany, Mother Firmata gave a farewell address in which she emphasized the elements that defined them as Poor Handmaids. She told her congregation to embrace humility and poverty, to be grateful for small things, and to avoid free associations with lay people. She reminded them to help each other and to obey superiors as if they represent the will of God. Finally she reminded them of the importance of communal prayer and devotions, concluding: "Sisters, adhere to the simple interior spirit. See to it that it remains in the congregation. Whether in America, Holland, Bohemia or Germany, as long as the spirit remains all will go well." As Mother Firmata departed the convent in Donaldson, the postulants and novices lined the hallway holding United States and German flags to symbolize the unity between the two countries.[33] The chronicler expressed the importance of this visit when she wrote: "Thanks be to God that the dear Reverend Mother visited the American sisters. Now we are certainly all united in love."[34] The mother general's visit renewed the ties between America and Germany and reinforced the idea, especially among the American-born sisters, that they were connected to a system of rules and obligations that originated in Europe and applied to the whole community.

In 1926, Sister Mary Felicissima Schichler began a series of murals for the motherhouse in Donaldson that demonstrated this unity. When she did this, she created images that expressed the ethnic consciousness of the Poor Handmaids in America. Several of the paintings depict events in the life of Mother Kasper and the growth of the community in Germany. One of them portrays the reception of the first sisters by Bishop Blum in 1851. The picture shows the sisters processing to meet the bishop in an idealized setting in Dernbach while the Virgin Mary looks down from heaven. In another painting, Sister Felicissima depicted the family tree of the Poor Handmaids. This tree has leaves that represent all the convents and hospitals staffed by the

32. Ibid., 329.

33. File "Ancilla Domini Chronicle, 1918–1926," CHJC 33/4, AUND, pages 31, 32.

34. File "Ancilla Domini Chronicles in German, 1893–1927," CHJC 33/2, AUND, page 321.

Bishop Blum receiving the first Poor Handmaids in 1851. Painting by Sister Mary Felicissima Schichler.

community in the 1920s. One branch includes those maintained in Germany, while another shows the growth of the community in the United States; two branches of the same tree. By the late 1920s, one of the things that could unite the order was a vision of a common history and a common mission. Even though the sisters spoke English and had American citizenship, they looked to their history in Germany to find meaning in their activities and spiritual journeys.

When Mother Kasper bid a tearful farewell to the first eight sisters who came to the United States, she may have wondered whether they would remember her. In fact, she laid the basis for an ethnic identity that created a transatlantic religious order. Her rules, governance, and example of holiness established firm guidelines for membership in the order. A certain level of acquiescence to German standards was required of sisters in America before 1930. The Poor Handmaids in the United States drew inspiration from those standards, as Sister Felicissima's murals attest. The sisters in America committed themselves to specific structures and beliefs that kept them engaged with their German counterparts. They found meaning in a German style of community building that anchored an ethnic identity.

"Nazareth College Leads the Way": Catholicism, Democracy, and Racial Justice at a Southern College, 1920–1955

Mary Linehan

"Nazareth College Leads the Way," proclaimed the Louisville Times on June 12, 1951, as it announced graduation ceremonies at the institution.[1] For the first time since 1904, African-American students in Kentucky earned degrees at a "white" college. Drawing on the institution's private and public records, this study examines the historical roots of racial prejudice at Nazareth and how it gave way to a tolerance grounded in political and spiritual values. It then considers the experiences of black students and evaluates this early attempt to integrate a southern college. Throughout, the Nazareth story will be located in the larger movement for racial justice in Catholic higher education and in the state of Kentucky.

The Sisters of Charity of Nazareth opened Kentucky's first college for women in 1920. By state law, admission was restricted to white women. The Day Law, passed in 1904, prohibited the teaching of students of different races in the same classroom.[2] Likewise, in 1920 most Catholic colleges excluded black students. Except for Xavier University in New Orleans, which was founded for African Americans, the majority of integrated Catholic institutions were in northern cities.[3] In spite of progressive views on other social issues, when it came to racial equality, the white women of Nazareth College reflected the views of their religion and their conservative southern community.[4]

From the start, racial prejudice prevailed on campus. An urban institution, Nazareth's center city location resulted in a diversity of neighbors, not all of whom the women regarded with good will. In 1926, one reported, "the sisters . . . derive much

---

1. *Louisville Times*, 12 June 1951.

2. John A. Hardin, *Fifty Years of Segregation: Black Higher Education in Kentucky, 1904–1954* (Lexington: University of Kentucky Press, 1997).

3. Philip Gleason, *Contending With Modernity: Catholic Higher Education in the Twentieth Century* (New York: Oxford, 1995), 155.

4. Anne Braden, *The Wall Between,* 2nd ed. (Knoxville: University of Tennessee Press, 1999). Pages 36–51 deal specifically with "The World of Segregated Louisville" in the 1950s.

amusement from the darkies in the alley . . . . a negro preacher and 'Will' an erstwhile collector of cartons."[5] In spite of this amusement, the sisters persistently tried to roust their neighbors. In the heart of the depression, the Louisville Chief of Police arranged for the eviction of the college's African-American neighbors. A sister wrote: "we will surely rejoice when we are rid of these hideous shacks and the terrible element who inhabit them."[6]

There were other expressions of racism at Nazareth during the 1920s and 1930s. The sisters called their driver, "our Darkey," their cook, "a poor old coon," and the children of these "faithful servants" were "little pickaninnies." At a Mardi Gras celebration, two sisters dressed as "colored twins" in blackface. Visiting the "colored school" the order operated at Saint Augustine's parish in the Portland neighborhood, a sister exclaimed, "it seemed as if little that was being taught was retained."[7] Student writing in the literary magazine featured black characters speaking in demeaning dialect. One 1932 piece was about Rastus, "'de slowes' lazies' nigger in de country."[8]

The women of Nazareth College were slow to develop a sympathetic or sensitive view on racial matters. Yet, as frequent victims of anti-Catholic bigotry and marginalized by gender and religion, they also understood themselves to be a despised minority culture. When a Jewish woman and two African-American servants attended the 1928 May Crowning, the sisters joked: "Ku Kluxers prick up your ears and don your sheets. At Nazareth College Catholics, Jews and Negroes actually consort in image worship."[9] This shared experience of discrimination may well have provided the foundation from which the Nazareth women could begin to work toward racial equality.

In the early 1940s, perhaps unconsciously and without an articulated rationale, a few hints of tolerance began to emerge. One indication of the changing racial climate was the college literary magazine. Stories written in dialect disappeared, although their replacements were still not all that might be hoped for. One praised opera singer Marian Anderson, said to "embody the spirit and character of the long-suffering Negro race, for they are a simple, humble people full of faith and hope."[10] Likewise, the sisters stopped referring to their staff in derogatory terms, eventually abandoning all mention of their race.[11] In the fall of 1940, in violation of the Day Law, the college offered a continuing education seminar that was opened to all women "of any creed or color."[12] The topic of the seminar, "The Christian Orientation of Life," suggests that

---

5. Annals, 31 May 1926. The Annals are the daily journals of the Sisters of Charity of Nazareth, Spalding University Archives, hereafter cited as SUA.

6. Ibid., 20 July 1934, SUA.

7. Ibid., 21 November 1925; 29 December 1925; 9 February 1935, SUA; 5 March 1935. Anna Blanche McGill, *The Sisters of Charity of Nazareth, Kentucky* (New York: Encyclopedia Press, 1917), 278. Berenice Greenwell, SCN, "Nazareth's Contribution to Education" (diss.: Fordham, 1933), 406.

8. *Pelican*, January 1928, 8; June 1932, 5; May 1935, 18, SUA. McGill, *The Sisters of Charity*, 288.

9. Annals, 1 May 1928, SUA.

10. *Pelican*, February 1943, SUA.

11. Annals, 21 January 1944; 13 April 1946; 9 May 1946; 21 September 1946, SUA.

12. *Louisville Times*, 15 September 1941.

the course was intended to proselytize, but, for the first time, the doors of Nazareth College were open to women of color. A similar evangelizing motive prompted the Sisters of Charity of Nazareth to open a "colored mission"—complete with a "training school for Negroes" and a fifty bed hospital—in Ensley, Alabama.[13]

Though Nazareth women expressed some tolerance for African Americans as the objects of charity and conversion, this in no way implied a commitment to racial equality. Catholic churches in Louisville were strictly segregated. When the pastor of one black parish asked permission to hold a day of recollection at the college he was flatly refused.[14] Similarly, a campus celebration of "Inter-American Unity" stressed the "common European cultural heritage" of North and South American peoples.[15] When the college chapter of the Catholic Students' Mission Crusade organized a debate on "The Church and The Negro" it was advertised as "one of the most controversial topics of our times."[16] Most telling of all, when the pastor of an African-American Catholic church spoke on campus in 1945, the first question he was asked was whether his congregation remained committed to maintaining segregated parishes.[17] His affirmative answer reassured many of the faculty and students. Only at the conclusion of World War II would a new generation of students emerge and demand racial equality at Nazareth College.

The institution's timid approach to justice was characteristic of Catholic higher education in the late 1930s and early 1940s. Organizations such as the Catholic Committee of the South, the Catholic Interracial Council, and the National Federation of Catholic College Students endeavored to focus attention on racial matters, but progress was not immediate. According to a 1941 survey, 87 institutions claimed to be dealing with racism in the classroom, yet fewer than a dozen offered courses on interracial relations. In 1944, more than 25 percent of Catholic colleges polled admitted to discriminating against African Americans in the admission process.[18]

Slowly, Catholic colleges began to integrate, but this was not without controversy. At Manhattanville, a northern women's college, the progressive president committed the college to racial equality in 1933. It took five years, however, to overcome alumnae opposition and enroll an African-American student. In 1944, St. Louis University became the first Catholic university in the South to experiment with integration. This happened despite the misgivings of the institution's president who attempted to

---

13. Annals, 9 March 1945; 10 March 1945; 5 October 1945; 28 August 1946. *Stub*, December 1945, 3. The *Stub* was the Nazareth College student newspaper. Some years only the month of publication was printed, SUA.

14. Ibid., 29 October 1945, SUA.

15. Ibid., 20 April 1945, 2, SUA.

16. Ibid., December 1945, 1, SUA.

17. Ibid., 20 April 1945, 4, SUA.

18. Gleason, *Contending With Modernity*, 155–156, 236. Since 1939, the Catholic Committee of the South united black and white Catholics to promote desegregation and effect "social change in the modern South through the use of religious principles." John B. Alberts, "Black Catholic Schools: The Josephite Parishes of New Orleans During the Jim Crow Era," *U.S. Catholic Historian* 12, n.1 (Winter 1994): 96.

segregate extra-curricular activities to affirm that equal educational opportunities did not presume the social equality of blacks and whites. After four years of student agitation on behalf of integration, the University of Notre Dame admitted its first black student during the Second World War.[19]

The conclusion of World War II hastened the movement toward racial toleration in all aspects of American life. In Louisville, Kentucky, this was particularly evident in higher education. In 1944, Gunnar Myrdal's *An American Dilemma* assailed racism in the United States asking how we could fight against hatred abroad while continuing to uphold discrimination at home. In Kentucky, as elsewhere, African-American veterans refused to accept this double standard and began to demand equality. In this former slave state, blacks voted and were politically active. They held elective office in counties with large black populations. Yet, public facilities—including schools—remained segregated.[20] Gaining access to more educational opportunities, and the social and economic mobility higher education promised, became a logical first priority for these reformers.

During the war, Louisville black activists mounted the first (unsuccessful) challenge to the Day Law.[21] At the time, Kentucky ranked 47th among 48 states in the percentage of college-educated residents. Only 4.7 percent of Kentuckians had completed four years of college, and only 1.6 percent of those were African American.[22] One result of this disparity was the scarcity of blacks qualified to teach in the state's 120 segregated school districts. Moreover, African Americans seeking advanced or professional degrees were forced to leave the state to complete their education. While whites could choose between five public and fifteen private colleges, black students were restricted to Louisville Municipal College or the Kentucky State College for Negroes in Frankfort. Neither of these institutions matched the resources available at white-designated colleges and universities. In a 1945 study, Kentucky ranked below neighboring southern states in the amount expended for the college education of African Americans. It provided half the amount Oklahoma budgeted for the same number of students.[23] It was nearly impossible for black students to receive a first-rate education in Kentucky. In spite of these facts, the state government—convinced that most whites opposed any form of integration—hid behind the fiction of "separate but equal" and remained committed to segregation.

As local black leaders continued to agitate against the Day Law, the women of Nazareth College moved closer to racial acceptance in their college community. From 1945 to 1950, Nazareth women developed a rationale for racial justice that would ultimately lead to integration of the college. Part of this justification was spiritual. Like their counterparts in Catholic colleges across the country, the women came to realize

---

19. Gleason, *Contending With Modernity*, 156, 238.
20. Hardin, *Fifty Years of Segregation*, 7.
21. Ibid., 73.
22. Ibid., 70, 108.
23. Ibid., 67, 80–81, 84, 90–91.

racial discrimination as a sinful moral offense.[24] They also came to see prejudice as incompatible with American democracy. Uniting these concerns under the auspices of Catholic Action, the faculty and students of Nazareth College sought to bring equality and justice to their community.

Sister Cyril Blubaugh, SCN, the generally conservative professor of home economics, was among the first to call for racial justice based on Catholic and democratic principles. Writing in the May 1946 college newsletter, she cited discrimination as one of the most important issues confronting family life and the home. Improved race relations called for "the thoughtful activity of every true Catholic woman." Therefore, Blubaugh maintained that the college must awaken in its students a keen awareness of current problems and inspire in them a "deep sense of responsibility as citizens, as Catholics, and as women."[25]

This charge was taken up by Reverend Alfred Horrigan, a popular philosophy professor. He challenged his students to realize the connection between Catholicism and racial justice. He did not attribute prejudice to basic wickedness. Rather, it was a "misunderstanding." Arguing that "brotherly love is the beautiful fruit of the tree of Christianity," Horrigan urged his students to pursue real cooperation between blacks and whites. They must not compromise with bigotry. "Love of God, love of family, and love of country," summed up the true Catholic position for Horrigan and any deviation—including racism—was a sin.[26]

Students writing in campus publications also advocated racial toleration based on Catholic and democratic principles. In October 1946, the editor of the student newspaper took up the topic. Kathleen Guinee argued that God placed an "immortal soul" in every human body and, through Baptism, every being became part of the "Mystical Body of Christ." As all Christians belonged to this Mystical Body, "no one has the right to subjugate another." Because "Heaven won't be segregated," she urged Nazareth students to join with African Americans and "prepare for our unified eternal life." Guinee saw American youth as uniquely advantaged and thus able to set an example for the rest of the world and "spread a fundamental knowledge of the principle of the equality of man."[27] Grounded in their religious faith and democratic liberty, Nazareth women might change the world through Catholic Action.

Although there were students who "would rather stand up on the busses than sit by a Negro," such racism was not the view of campus leaders.[28] In the late 1940s they joined with other Louisville students to improve racial understanding and work for social change. Such spiritually motivated activism among young people fit well with the ideas of Catholic Action. For more than ten years, this movement had worked to improve Catholic influence on society through social service.[29] Nazareth students

24. Gleason, *Contending With Modernity,* 236–237.
25. College newsletter, May 1946, SUA.
26. *Louisville Courier Journal*, 28 February 1946.
27. *Stub*, November 19462, SUA.
28. Ibid., 26 February 1948, 3; February 1949, 2, SUA.
29. Gleason, *Contending With Modernity*, 153–154.

already engaged in Catholic Action through the Sodality, the Catholic Students' Mission Crusade, the St. Vincent DePaul Society, the "colored mission" in Alabama, and the summer schools they operated in Appalachia. Combating racism in their own community seemed the next logical step.

In November 1945, student leaders from Nazareth College—along with representatives from the Young Men's Christian Association, the Young Men's Hebrew Association, Flaget Memorial Catholic High School, Catholic Colored High School, and the all-black Central High School—formed Youth In Action (YIA). The group aimed to transform the "mental attitudes between the races" for a "reciprocal understanding" of racial problems. Drawing inspiration from the Declaration of Independence and the United Nations' Charter, and from their religious faiths, the students resolved "to treat all men with the respect due them as children of God and to influence others by our word and example."[30]

As specific means to accomplish its aims, YIA demanded that the same educational opportunities be made available to all students. This was not a clear denunciation of the Day Law, for the students claimed "this does not mean there should be no segregation." Yet, they also urged the opening of economic opportunities and professional training for all people; equal and sufficient medical care for all; the lifting of racial and religious restrictions barring persons from public buildings, parks, and places of amusement; and the encouragement of intercultural education throughout the school system.[31]

In the spring of 1946, as the first step toward its long-range goals, Youth In Action sponsored a series of lectures and discussions. Prominent civic leaders—black and white, lay and religious—spoke on such topics as "How the Negro Feels About His Position in Society," "The True Catholic Position," and "Political and Economic Problems of the Negro."[32] After a presentation, the students led a discussion on how Louisvillians might respond. By the fall of 1946, these discussions led to a weekly radio program, "The Junior Roundtable," through which the students promoted their ideas of racial justice.

The YIA organization was still quite conservative, dedicated to dialogue rather than direct action as a means of achieving change. Although they were committed to improved education for African-Americans, they were not yet ready to move beyond "separate but equal" schools. In early 1948, when Louisville black activists mounted another challenge to the Day Law, YIA was conspicuously silent. While black students naively celebrated the revolutionary possibilities of YIA—it "may mean the difference between this world's becoming one great race or one great mass of poverty and suffering"—Nazareth students drew something else from their involvement.[33] Teenagers, raised in an environment where their schools, neighborhoods, and

30. *Louisville Courier Journal*, 27 January 1946.
31. Ibid., 27 January 1946.
32. Ibid., 13 February 1946. Annals, 15 January 1947; 21 May 1947.
33. *Stub*, 17 April 1947, 1, SUA.

recreational activities were racially restricted, the white women of YIA gloried in the opportunity to meet people of another race. As Patricia Mattingly explained: "I've not only found my cure for a narrow mind, but I've also discovered a whole new world, a few of whose cultured and talented people I am proud to know are my friends."[34] From this basis of friendship, Nazareth students would soon be ready to challenge the Day Law.

By 1947, Youth In Action had 25 members and a faculty sponsor, Sister Anita Horrigan, of Nazareth College. These students all belonged to the Catholic Students' Mission Crusade, the most important extra-curricular activity on campus. YIA membership also included class officers, the newspaper editors, and the college's top ranked students.[35] Their views may have been controversial and unsophisticated, but these campus leaders were in a position to influence campus thought and activities.

Each spring, the various student clubs at Nazareth organized an Interracial Justice Week in tandem with Brotherhood Week sponsored by the National Conference of Christians and Jews. These observances included presentations by African Americans, panel discussions, and writing or poster contests.[36] The speakers often came from Catholic Colored High School or were Catholic women who attended the segregated Louisville Municipal College. These speakers, along with friendships forged through YIA, personalized prejudice and increasingly made Nazareth students aware of their college's complicity in upholding the Jim Crow South. Moreover, a state law which barred their black friends from attending Nazareth College was both unchristian and undemocratic and must be opposed.

By May 1948, the students were ready to take more forceful action on behalf of racial justice. Senior Martha Ann Yarber, a YIA member, represented Nazareth at the annual meeting of the National Federation of Catholic College Students (NFCCS). Four years earlier the federation appointed a commission dedicated to interracial justice.[37] Yarber, a NFCCS officer, now demanded action. She joined in sponsoring a resolution, "that [NFCCS] must recommend a standard policy of non-discrimination in regard to race, color, and creed of students in Catholic institutions of higher learning."[38] This galvanized the Nazareth students, and they began to demand that the administration defy the Day Law and enroll African-American women.[39]

The students' demand coincided with developments in Catholic higher education and in the state of Kentucky. Early in 1950, the National Catholic Education Association called upon Catholic colleges to end racial segregation in education and take charge of efforts for equal educational opportunities for all people. The Nazareth community applauded this resolution.[40] Weeks later, the African-American state

---

34. Ibid., 17 April 1947, 3, SUA.

35. Ibid., October 1946, 1, SUA.

36. Ibid., 27 February 1947, 3; 26 February 1948, 1; February 1949, 4, SUA.

37. Gleason, *Contending With Modernity*, 236, SUA.

38. *Stub*, May 1948, 1, SUA.

39. Ibid., February 1949, 2, SUA.

40. Ibid., January 1950, 1, SUA. *Catholic Telegraph-Register*, 28 April 1950.

representative from Louisville's 42nd House District, Jesse Lawrence, proposed an amendment to the Day Law which would permit black students to attend "white" institutions *if* courses of equal quality were not available at Kentucky State College for Negroes. His bill passed by a 50–16 margin. Sponsored in the Senate by white Louisvillian, Leon Shaikun, the amended Day Law passed without debate.[41]

Louisville's three Catholic colleges—Nazareth, Ursuline, and Bellarmine—acted at once. They issued a statement opening their schools "from this time on" to people of color. They emphasized the spiritual and political roots of their action: "we wish to express our thorough satisfaction that the legal barriers against the full application of the principles of Christianity and democracy in the field of higher education in our state have now been removed."[42] At the same time, the University of Louisville voted not to admit black undergraduates. They argued that Louisville Municipal College offered the same courses. The Catholics quickly moved to distinguish themselves. The three college presidents responded: "the colleges which we represent offer as part of every course of study a number of semester hours in religion and scholastic philosophy . . . therefore . . . none of our courses can be said to be offered in a complete sense at the Kentucky State College for Negroes."[43]

Although all three Catholic colleges vowed to desegregate at the same time, most of the responsibility for implementing this policy fell to Nazareth College. Within a week of the Day Law amendment, they had admitted twenty-five African-American women to matriculate in the fall of 1950. Ursuline accepted just two women, while Bellarmine enrolled three men.[44] In a statement of their own, the Sisters of Charity of Nazareth stressed the connection between racial justice and spiritual and political values which had been a growing part of campus culture during the past ten years. The sisters wrote: "we wish to reaffirm our faith in the basic principles of Christian social philosophy that all human rights derive from man's spiritual development and his supernatural destiny as a child of God. When the right to an intellectual and spiritual development which is the proper concern of higher education is curtailed by the physical accident of race, there is implicit in such curtailment a materialistic philosophy of life which is intolerable in a Christian and democratic society."[45]

Louisville, as a whole, seemed divided on the sisters' decision. The local newspaper claimed that the city should congratulate itself for being in the "forefront of Southern cities" in its efforts to "equalize educational opportunities for all its citizens." Yet, the liberal *Courier-Journal* also approved of the secular university's resolve not to admit black students.[46] The sisters, victims of Klan violence in the past, made no record of any opposition to their integration plans. The diocesan newspaper, however, reported:

41. Hardin, *Fifty Years of Segregation*, 100.
42. *Louisville Courier-Journal*, 19 April 1950. *Catholic Telegraph-Register*, 28 April 1950.
43. Ibid., 19 April 1950.
44. Ibid., 19 April 1950; 22 April 1950. *Louisville Catholic Record*, 6 June 1951.
45. Ibid., 20 April 1950.
46. Ibid., 20 April 1950; 23 April 1950.

Staff of the Pelican *literary magazine. (All photos in this article are courtesy: The Spalding University Archives)*

"God has permitted the sisters the good fortune of being criticized for their actions in . . . striving to apply Christian principles to racial problems."[47]

Within the college itself, integration peacefully proceeded. One local newspaper reported that the 1950–1951 academic year "passed uneventfully" with no "instances" and none of the "dire consequences" predicted by alarmists. The editor claimed the acceptance of integration at Nazareth was "unprecedented" in any part of the country "to say nothing of a state south of the Mason-Dixon line."[48] The college newspaper frequently printed photos showing interracial groups of students at prayer in the chapel, studying, eating in the cafeteria, waiting for the bus, and playing ping pong.[49] Such scenes were remarkable in a city that—apart from Nazareth College—remained strictly segregated. There were few other places in Louisville where blacks and whites could live, work, socialize, and eat together.[50]

One third of Nazareth's first year class in 1950–1951 were African-Americans.[51] That such a large-scale integration could happen so smoothly reflects the depth of the religious and political values that underlie the opening of the college to women

47. *Louisville Record*, 12 September 1952.
48. *Louisville Times*, 12 September 1951.
49. *Stub*, October 1950, 1; February 1951, 3; May 1951, 3, SUA.
50. For more on segregation in Louisville, see Braden, *The Wall Between*.
51. Annals, 17 September 1951, SUA. *Louisville Times*, 12 September 1951.

1954 Social Science majors.

of color and the sincerity of the student friendships developed through Youth In Action and other interracial ventures.

In June of 1951, Nazareth College granted degrees to two African-American women. Patricia Lauderdale, a Social Science major who hoped to become "a successful business person," was a graduate of Central High School. In 1948, while a student at Municipal College, Lauderdale spoke on "the Catholic Negro" during Nazareth's Interracial Justice Week. She convinced many of the white students that the Day Law was immoral. As a Nazareth student, she participated in the Interracial Club (the successor to YIA) and the Dance Club. Barbara Simmons Miller was also a graduate of Central High School and already had a Mus. B. at the University of Michigan. She added a B.S. in Library Science from Nazareth and was satisfied enough with her experience that she returned for a graduate degree. Later, Miller became the first African-American faculty member at the college.[52]

The first five years of integration at Nazareth College, 1950–1955, witnessed other firsts which give the impression that black women were welcome and adjusting well to

52. *Stub*, 26 February 1948, 1; May 1951, 3–4, SUA. After earning her degree from an integrated college, Barbara Miller became a librarian in the segregated Louisville Free Public Library system. In 1970, she successfully challenged racial discrimination in apartment rentals in Louisville. In 1971, she received the Caritas Medal as an outstanding alumnus of Spalding [Nazareth] College.

Joyce Charleston, Frances Clausell, Rubenna Dickerson, June Anderson

the college. In 1950, Charlotte Williamson, a Central High School graduate, was elected Vice President of the first year class. In the academic year 1954–1955, three of the four senior class officers were African American. The same year, a black woman, Evelyn Morris, was elected president of Nazareth's most prestigious student organization, the Catholic Students' Mission Crusade.

Integration at Nazareth was cultural as well as spatial. Individual black women found niches for themselves on campus. The six black women who received diplomas in 1955 all excelled as members of the college community. Rubenna Dickerson, a Social Science major and a four-year member of the drama club, was Secretary of the senior class and also served as president of the Interracial Club. June Anderson, a Social Science major and member of the the a *cappella* choir, was accepted for graduate work at Indiana University. Joyce Charleston majored in Home Economics and was president of the Home Ec club as well as treasurer of the senior class. Frances Clausell, an Elementary Education major, represented Nazareth in Louisville's all-college talent show. Joyce Dawson, also a Home Economics major was twice elected as a class officer. Nursing major Blossie Mayo played forward on the basketball team, sang with a *cappella,* and in 1953 was one of five finalists in the balloting for Holly Belle, queen of the Christmas Ball.

After 1955, however, the presence and acceptance of black students at Nazareth College declined. From 1956 to 1963, only three African Americans served as class officers out of 92 women elected to such positions.[53] During this period, photographs of women of color all but disappeared from college publications. When black students at Nazareth did make the news it was generally for academic success or for the workings of the Interracial Club which became the unofficial home of African-American women on the Nazareth College campus.[54] Although enrollment reports did not always include race, as the number of full-time day students increased from 168 in 1951, to 220 in 1957, to 688 in 1967, the percentage of black women in the student body dropped from almost forty percent to less than three percent.[55]

There are several reasons for this precipitous decline in the number of black students. First, the generation of white students who participated in Youth in Action and other Catholic Action organizations graduated. Their successors appear to have been more interested in the social side of college life than in the political and religious implications of segregation. As beauty pageants, cheerleading for Bellarmine College, and participating in the Kentucky Derby festival came to dominate campus culture, black students—and more radical whites—may have felt less welcome at Nazareth.[56] Moreover, by the late 1950s, African Americans had access to less costly academic opportunities. In 1951, Louisville Municipal College closed and its students were allowed to transfer to the University of Louisville. In 1956, the presidents of the state's regional colleges agreed to integrate their campuses.[57] Finally, in an effort to keep "white" schools white, state officials at last began to provide adequate financial support to Kentucky State. As the resources of the Frankfort institution improved, many black collegians—loyal to the heritage and tradition of Kentucky State—made it their first choice for higher education.[58]

More puzzling—given the heartfelt spiritual and patriotic commitment to racial justice and the bravery that led the Sisters of Charity of Nazareth to integrate their institution—is the silence of the faculty and administration. Not only did the declining number of African-American students pass without comment, the sisters also failed to publicly or privately acknowledge the larger struggle for civil rights. Not a word was recorded about the Brown decision, Montgomery, Little Rock, Greensboro, Birmingham, the integration of southern state universities, the activism of SNCC in the South, or the 1957 desegregation of Louisville public schools. When Cassius Clay, "a negro boy who works in our library after school," appeared in the 1958 Golden Gloves tournament, the sisters "cheered him on to victory."[59] In 1963, two sisters judged a cake contest sponsored by the *Louisville Defender* as part of the centennial celebration

---

53. *Stub*, May 1957, 2; 28 April 1961, 3, SUA.

54. Ibid., April 1961, 3; 28 May 1962, 1, SUA.

55. Annals, 17 November 1951; 2 October 1957. *Stub*, 23 February 1967, 3, SUA.

56. Helen Lefkowitz Horowitz, *Campus Life: Undergraduate Culture from the End of the Eighteenth Century to the Present* (Chicago: University of Chicago Press, 1987), 229, discusses the hostile reaction to activist students on campus in the 1950s.

57. Hardin, *Fifty Years of Segregation*, 102, 110.

58. Ibid., 111–115.

59. Annals, 17 January 1958, SUA.

of the Emancipation Proclamation.[60] Otherwise, the sisters remained silent on everything pertaining to race. It was as if by integrating the college in 1950 they had done *their* part. Discrimination and hatred off campus—especially radical and controversial movements—were not their concern.[61] This attitude did not change until 1964 when John F. Kennedy's death inspired, and Vatican II reforms made possible, a new commitment to social justice among the faculty and students of Nazareth College.

It would be wrong to interpret the integration of Nazareth College as a failure. Although the initial enthusiasm of the students was not maintained, and even though this experiment did not lead to more widespread social justice activism, the Nazareth women—black and white, students and sisters—did indeed lead the way. Their courage and faith-based commitment to interracial acceptance would be replicated by Catholic and Protestant women throughout the South in the 1960s, and their peaceful desegregation of a southern college modeled a new possibility for other institutions in the region.[62] Moreover, never again would the doors of this college be closed to African Americans. Even though their numbers declined, black students never disappeared. From 1950 on, there existed in Louisville at least one place where Christian ideals and democratic principles combined to fracture the color line. In Louisville, Nazareth College led the way.

---

60. Annals, 5 November 1963, SUA.

61. Braden, *The Wall Between*, 320 discusses the "extreme hostility" in Louisville to "subversive" civil rights activists after 1954.

62. Hardin, *Fifty Years of Segregation*, 9. For the experiences of Protestant women in the 1960s who were motivated to participate in civil rights activities because of their religious beliefs see Sara Evans, *Personal Politics: The Roots of Women's Liberation in the Civil Rights Movement and the New Left* (New York: Knopf, 1979), 28–35.

Beyond the Immigrant Church: Gays and Lesbians and the Catholic Church in San Francisco, 1977–1987

Jeffrey M. Burns

The Archdiocese of San Francisco underwent a profound demographic shift during the 1970s and 1980s. Following the Immigration Reform Act of 1965, waves of new immigrants arrived in the city—Mexicans, Salvadorans, Nicaraguans, Guatemalans, Vietnamese, Koreans, Chinese, Filipinos, Somoans, Tongans and others. At the same time, many of the older immigrant groups, namely the Irish and Italians, had begun moving to the suburbs. By 2000, the Asian population surpassed the white population in the city. Included among these new immigrants were large numbers of Catholics. By 2000, Filipinos made up about one-fourth of all Catholics in the Archdiocese of San Francisco. The Church in San Francisco greeted these immigrants with a new model of assimilation "cultural pluralism"—the Church was to act not simply as an agent of Americanization; it was to respect and nurture the cultural expressions of faith the new immigrants brought with them from their native lands.

Another demographic change proved to be more challenging. Following World War II, a small homosexual subculture began to develop in San Francisco. By 1980 some estimates suggested that there were 120,000 gay and lesbian men and women in the city, just less than twenty percent of the city's total population. San Francisco was reputed to have the largest, most concentrated, most open gay community in the United States. The most concentrated area of settlement was known as the Castro. In 1978, the growing political power of the gay community was reflected in the election of the first openly gay city supervisor, Harvey Milk.

The growth of the gay community presented enormous pastoral problems for the Church in San Francisco. The gays could not be treated as any other minority. A "national" parish for gays and lesbians could not be established as had been done for previous non-immigrant minorities such as African-Americans. Whereas cultural pluralism could be used to greet the new immigrants, a "moral pluralism" could not be adopted to accommodate the gay community. Thus, there is the problem, how to minister effectively to the gay Catholic community while remaining faithful to the

Church's traditional teaching on marriage and sexuality, which condemned the gay lifestyle as sinful?

This essay focuses on the decade 1977 to 1987, the first decade of the episcopacy of John Raphael Quinn, the sixth archbishop of San Francisco (1977–1995). During that decade, Quinn and the church in San Francisco worked to accommodate gay and lesbian Catholics while upholding the traditional teaching against homosexuality. The accommodation did not come easy.

Dignity

The first significant gay Catholic ministry began prior to Quinn's arrival: in January 1973, Dignity, a support group for gay and lesbian Catholics, began celebrating mass at St. Peter's parish hall in San Francisco at 3:00 pm on Sunday afternoons. When news of Dignity's presence became public, as a result of a *San Francisco Examiner* article, a storm of protest broke out. In response, the archdiocesan newspaper, *The Monitor*, ran a rather surprising editorial. While it reiterated the Church's opposition to homosexuality, it cautioned that homosexuality was a complex problem, and that the homosexual had to be treated like everyone else: ". . . our homosexual brothers and sisters . . . are no more virtuous or promiscuous, no more Christ-like or exploitive than any other group of people. . . . Charity and love must be our motives in our dialogue with homosexual Christians…"[1] The editorial established the contours of what would become the basic archdiocesan policy over the next fifteen years.

Archbishop John R. Quinn

John R. Quinn arrived in San Francisco in 1977. He was an alumnus of the North American College and Gregorian University in Rome. He had served several years as professor and rector at the diocesan seminary in San Diego before being appointed auxiliary bishop of San Diego in 1967. In 1972, he became bishop of Oklahoma City and Tulsa, and in 1973, he became the first archbishop of Oklahoma City. Little in Quinn's past prepared him for the collision between the Catholic Church and the gay community he encountered in San Francisco.

Tensions between the Church and the gay community multiplied shortly after Quinn's arrival. In November 1978, Mayor George Moscone and Supervisor Harvey Milk were assassinated by former Supervisor Dan White. Much was made of White's Catholic school training (he had attended Catholic grade school and high school) and

---

1. "Editorial: Homosexuality," *San Francisco Monitor* (hereafter referred to as *SFM*), (January 25, 1973): 4.

the fact that the district he represented was Irish Catholic. In his chronicle of the assassination, Randy Shilts easily associates the term "Irish Catholic" with homophobia, and suggests that the gay influx into the Castro area resulted in a massive Irish Catholic exodus.[2] From the perspective of many in the gay community, to be Catholic was to be homophobic, and many suspected Catholics of being sympathetic to Dan White.

1979 saw the creation of one of San Francisco's most notorious groups, and one that grated on the sensibilities of many Catholics—the Sisters of Perpetual Indulgence. The sisters consisted of a group of gay men, who publicly donned the religious habits of Catholic women religious. The sisters soon became quite visible in the Castro area and at major gay events and celebrations around the city. In 1982, the sisters set off howls of indignation when they attended an interfaith prayer service at St. Mary's Cathedral. The gay community newspaper, *The Bay Area Reporter*, reported that the sisters did not intend their presence to be an affront: "The Sisters state that they are emulating, not mocking the Roman Catholic nuns. Their comment is they honor the spiritual and feminist quality which is represented by the nuns."[3] The good intentions of the sisters were doubted by most Catholics who found the names of sisters such as Sister Hysterectoria and Sister Boom Boom totally outrageous and demeaning to the Catholic sisterhood. *The Monitor* concluded, "The organization, their names, and their use of religious habits is an affront to religious women and Catholics in general."[4]

By early 1980, Archbishop Quinn felt the need to articulate clearly the Church's teaching on homosexuality. On May 5 he issued a "Pastoral Letter on Homosexuality."[5] In a carefully nuanced text, Quinn stressed the complexities involved in pastoral ministry to homosexuals. He clearly restated the Church's opposition to homosexual activity, but noted, homosexual "orientation" was not condemned. Catholics were urged to stand up against violence directed toward gays, and to protect gay civil rights, however, "To agree that the persecution and harassment of homosexuals is incompatible with the Gospel is, therefore, not to say that the Church and society should be neutral about homosexual activity." Nonetheless, "While it is clear that the Scriptures condemn homosexual behavior, this does not imply any justification for the exploitation of the homosexual or injury to his or her dignity as a human person. Thus there is a clear difference between the acceptance of homosexual persons as worthy of respect and as having human rights, and approval of the homosexual lifestyle . . . Homosexual behavior cannot be viewed as an acceptable form of behavior morally or socially." Even so, homosexuals were persons who had to be provided "sound pastoral care," they were no different than other Christians, who daily had to struggle to overcome

---

2. Randy Shilts, *The Mayor of Castro Street: The Life and Times of Harvey Milk* (New York: St. Martin's Press, 1982), 185.

3. "Sisters of Perpetual Indulgence Cause Pleasure and Pain," *Bay Area Reporter* (hereafter referred to as *BAR*), (July 15, 1982): 9.

4. "Editorial" *SFM*, (November 11, 1982): 4.

5. All quotes taken from the pastoral letter. Copy in the Archives of the Archdiocese of San Francisco.

sin and "become rooted in the person of Jesus Christ." They should avail themselves of the sacraments of the Eucharist and reconciliation in their struggle. The Church had to be pastorally sensitive to this struggle and assist all people to holiness. What was particularly striking was the pastoral tone of the letter. Quinn concluded with warning against divisiveness and recriminations. Citing Ephesians, he counseled, "Take heart . . . Get rid of all bitterness, all passion and anger, harsh words, slander, and malice of every kind. In place of these, be kind to one another, compassionate and mutually forgiving, just as God has forgiven you in Christ . . ."

Quinn's pastoral letter was hailed by many for its pastoral sensitivity, but was criticized by conservatives for allegedly soft pedaling the Church's condemnation of homosexuality; many in the gay community regarded it as the same old church line. The *Bay Area Reporter (BAR)* responded with an article entitled, "SF Catholics Condemn Homo-Sex," which expressed "amazement" that the topic had been addressed at all. However, the *BAR* suggested that Quinn had condemned homosexuality in order to receive a "major papal appointment." It noted that to advance in the contemporary Church, one could not be accused of being "soft on gays."[6] In ensuing issues of the *BAR*, several letters to the editor criticized Quinn, one suggesting that he would do better by facing the issue of "gay priests."[7] Two weeks later, the *BAR* did run a front page story citing the response of the New Ways Ministry in Washington, D.C., which called Quinn's letter "inadequate." It did, however, see the letter as "an encouraging sign," which at least noted the complexity of the issue involved, and admitted there were no easy answers.[8]

Surprisingly, Quinn's letter evoked no response in the pages of the archdiocesan newspaper.

The Task Force on Gay/Lesbian Issues

In May 1981, the Archdiocesan Commission on Social Justice established a Task Force on Gay/Lesbian Issues to address the problem of increasing violence against gays in San Francisco and to suggest ways of combating its increase. Fourteen members were appointed—two priests, one brother, one woman religious, five laymen, and five laywomen. Included in the group were several gay and lesbian men and women, including the co-chair of Dignity San Francisco. Another appointee was the co-founder of the support group Parents and Friends of Gays. Most members were involved in pastoral ministry, education, or counseling. The task force was chaired by layman Kevin Gordon, a therapist and theologian, who had received a doctorate in systematic theology at the Union Theological Seminary in New York City.

6. "SF Catholics Condemn Homo-Sex," *BAR*, (May 22, 1980): 1.

7. Loretta Humphries, "An Open Letter to Archbishop Quinn," *BAR*, (June 19, 1980).

8. "Catholic Gay Group Calls Quinn Pastoral on Homosexuality 'Inadequate,'" *BAR*, (June 19, 1980): 1.

After consulting for more than a year, on July 29, 1982, the Task Force approved a report entitled *Homosexuality and Social Justice*. The Archdiocesan Commission on Social Justice accepted the report as a "working document," which, as the Executive Director of the Commission, Thomas Ambrogi, stressed in his introduction, "is not an official document of the Archdiocese itself."[9] Since its foundation in 1964, the Commission had operated as a "semi-autonomous" body within the Archdiocese. It was permitted to make public statements that did not necessarily reflect the mind of the archbishop. Such was the case with the Task Force Report.

Archbishop Quinn was under the impression that the Task Force was to focus solely on violence against gays, and cautioned the Commission to "go slowly" on this sensitive issue. He was quite surprised with the resulting 150-page report, which went far beyond the Task Force's mandate. The radical document, to be published by the Commission, did address the problem of violence against gays, but it went far beyond that. At the heart of the document was a frontal assault on the Church's traditional condemnation of homosexuality. The report called for the Church to develop "a new, positive sexual ethic" that would incorporate the gift of gay sexuality. It argued that church teaching condemned gays to a celibate lifestyle that failed to acknowledge healthy and spirit-filled gay sexual relationships. It prevented gays from leading fully integrated lives. The report argued that it was ridiculous for the Church to argue for gay civil rights while it condemned gay sexual activity. Indeed, in condemning gay sexuality, the Church contributed to violence against gays, by legitimizing discrimination. In that light, the Church had to be regarded as an "oppressor." The Church was guilty of promoting homophobia, and sexism as well. As the report asserted, ". . . the domination, male control and repression of women basically underlies the oppression of all homosexual persons . . ."

If the assault on the traditional sexual ethic was not bold enough, the report also attacked its sponsor, Archbishop Quinn. One recommendation advised: "That the Archdiocese representatives refrain from making empirically unsupported, and inflammatory statements about homosexuality such as contained in the *Pastoral Letter on Homosexuality*: 'A normalization of homosexuality could only too easily foster and make more public homosexual behavior with the result of eroding the meaning of family.'"

At a press conference, Task Force chair Kevin Gordon stated that it was appropriate for this report to be published in San Francisco noting, "If not here, then where?" He went on to stress that the Church faced a "moment of incredible opportunity" and it should "seize the moment."[10] In another interview, Gordon claimed the report "challenged the Church to squarely face the issue of human sexuality in our Church, precisely as a justice issue demanding open and sustained dialogue."[11] Ambrogi concurred,

---

9. Thomas Ambrogi in *Homosexuality and Social Justice: Report of the Task Force on Gay/Lesbian Issues* (San Francisco: Commission on Social Justice, 1982), iii.

10. Quoted in "Report Issued on Homosexuality and Church in San Francisco," *SFM*, (September 16, 1982): 1.

11. Quoted in Allen White, "Bishop Sits on Hot Report," *BAR*, (September 9, 1982): 5.

though he did not agree with all the report's recommendations. "We need to listen to the voices of Gays and Lesbians and not just hierarchy or clergy,"[12] and "the Commission's main motivation was to establish a forum wherein the Church and the City could hear the real voices and the real experiences of homosexuals."[13]

As might be expected, the gay community, as represented in the *Bay Area Reporter*, hailed the report. *BAR* reporter Allen White, in an article entitled "Local Catholics Issue Revolutionary Report," wrote that the report "has come flying out of the closet of the Roman Catholic Archdiocese with a stinging, driving force." Further, he noted, "Though not an official statement of the Archdiocese, it is remarkable that the document has been released."[14]

More surprising was the official Catholic response—though Quinn privately fumed that he had been "betrayed," in public he made no immediate comment, but allowed the report to be debated. Archdiocesan spokesman Father Miles O'Brien Riley observed, "The Church must be viewed as a circle of viewpoints and not a pyramid." The archdiocesan newspaper gave extensive coverage to the report and published an editorial signed by editor Father John P. Penebsky entitled, "Will We Listen?" The editorial predicted accurately that the report would evoke a wide variety of reactions, from horror to delight, but counseled that the report should be read "thoughtfully and thoroughly . . . ; it is a document important to the life of the Church in the Archdiocese." As such, the document should not be lightly dismissed, nor should it be exploited by agents of change. "We do not agree with many of the Report's findings and recommendations. On the other hand, we respect the report for what it is—a working document voicing the real feelings of real people who have had the courage to speak out . . . . [W]e hope the report will be read, studied, discussed, and, yes, prayed over . . ."[15]

Over the course of the next several months, *The Monitor* published a wide variety of responses from denunciations to support. Many expressed "shock" at the report; others concurred with the assessment of one reader who called the report "pure garbage." Many questioned the orthodoxy of the report. Others, however, took the report as a hopeful sign, with the chair of Dignity San Francisco writing to thank the Task Force.

Archbishop Quinn was slow to respond publicly. The report put Quinn in an extremely awkward position. To endorse the report was unthinkable, but so was repressing the report—the year-long consultative process had to be respected. Repression might cause a severe backlash that would create problems of its own. Over the course of the next eight months Quinn progressively distanced himself from the report.

---

12. Quoted in Allen White, "Local Catholics Issue Revolutionary Report," *BAR*, (September 23, 1982): 4.

13. "Report Issued . . ."*SFM*, (September 16, 1982): 1.

14. White, "Local Catholics . . .," 4.

15. John P. Penebsky, "Editorial: Will We Listen?" *SFM*, (September 16, 1982).

In December, Quinn appointed a new Director of the Commission on Social Justice, the much respected Monsignor Peter G. Armstrong, long-time head of the Catholic Youth Organization. Ambrogi remained as Executive Secretary. Armstrong immediately began to qualify the Church's support for the report. "[I]n moral terms, we as Church, can only go so far, we have to reach out within the framework of the teaching of the Church." Armstrong was enunciating the Archbishop's views. In a letter to all the priests in the Archdiocese, Quinn made his most specific response to date, but within the larger context of setting priorities for the CSJ. "[T]he Commission will have to come to grips with the fact that the Task Force report contains much that is contrary to . . . the moral, ethical, and doctrinal teaching of the Church. At the same time those things in the report which are contrary to the teaching of the Church are nevertheless an expression of the sincerely held views of some people. For this reason, of course, we should be prepared to listen . . . Nevertheless, no matter how sincerely those views are held, it is imperative that we always be faithful to the truth and to the moral teaching of the Church."[16] Quinn did express his fear that the "Task Force has appeared to take on a life of its own." It would be necessary to rein them in.

On January 19, 1983, the Commission on Social Justice met amid rumors that the Task Force was to be disbanded. By a vote of 3 to 8, the Commission decided not to disband the Task Force. Armstrong, however, bluntly assailed the report, "[M]y personal and strong opinion is that this Report is an attack on the Church."[17] He made it clear that the public should be made aware that the report was not an official statement of the Church.

The Commission on Social Justice met again on February 17 to "clarify" the relation of the report to the Commission. By a vote of 7 to 2, the Commission agreed to accept the report as a "working document," and called for continuing "dialogue." At the same time, however, they endorsed a resolution that asserted "some views expressed in the Task Force report are clearly incompatible with that doctrine [of the Church] and moral teaching."[18] Several members of the Task Force, led by Kevin Gordon, felt they had not been given a fair hearing at the meeting and that they were being "railroaded." Gordon fumed that the Commission's action "short circuits dialogue," and accused chancery officials of "trying to whittle away the work we have accomplished . . . They are showing ruthless disrespect for the commissioners."[19]

Then on May 19, the Archdiocesan Senate of Priests issued a report entitled, "Ministry and Sexuality in the Archdiocese of San Francisco," directed to those involved in ministry with homosexuals. The priests' report was officially accepted as archdiocesan

---

16. Archbishop John Quinn quoted in "Monsignor Armstrong, Archbishop Quinn Discuss Priorities of Commission on Social Justice," *SFM*, (December 16, 1982): 3.

17. Monsignor Peter G. Armstrong quoted in "Social Justice Commission Meets under New Chairman, Discusses Gay, Lesbian Issues Report," *SFM*, (January 27, 1982): 1.

18. "Commission on Social Justice Clarifies Task Force, Report" *SFM*, (February 24, 1983): 1.

19. George Mendenhall, "Gay Task Force Still Nettles S.F. Archdiocese," *BAR*, (March 3, 1983): 2.

policy by Archbishop Quinn. The report was a remarkably progressive and innovative document, which would have been regarded as a major development in ministry to homosexuals had it not followed the Task Force Report. The forty-page report called on ministers to be compassionate and non-judgmental in dealing with homosexuals. It made at least four significant breakthroughs, though it repeatedly reaffirmed traditional church sexual teaching that sexual activity was acceptable only within the married state.

First, the report debunked many of the commonly held stereotypes of gay people: gays were not attracted to children, were not easily identified, were no more promiscuous than others, were in all professions, were not "mentally disordered," nor could they overcome their orientation through willpower.

Second, "The homosexual orientation is not held to be a sinful condition, as with heterosexuality, it represents the situation in which one finds oneself, the starting point for one's response to Christ's call to perfection. Responding to this call does not mean that one must change this orientation. Rather, it entails living out the demands of chastity within that orientation."

Third, and most remarkably, the report advocated a policy of "gradualism" in counseling gay men and women. It is worth quoting at length:

> Chastity is always the responsibility and goal of the Christian life . . . the homosexual person should not be surprised by periodic tensions and some relapses . . .

> It is [the] need for closeness and intimacy that leads the homosexual person to seek a stable relationship with another person. Homosexual people fall in love. And as long as this is so, sexual activity may occur . . .

> Objectively, the Church teaches that homosexual activity in such unions . . . is morally unacceptable. The principle of gradualism recognizes this fact and assists the person toward a progressive assimilation of the Church's ethical values. Pastoral judgments can never be made in the abstract, therefore, but always within the circumstances of this person's life . . .

> It is . . . important to carefully interpret the meaning of the sexual activity in this person's life: that is, to understand the pattern of life in which such activity takes place and to take into consideration the meanings these sexual acts have for different people . . . [M]inistry in this area demands an awareness that purification and growth in holiness come about only gradually . . .

> Any failure, then, to totally realize at this moment everything that one is called to be and to do does not negate the possibility of future success. We are all sinners who at times violate our best moral convictions, but we can be healed and forgiven.

Finally, the report noted that the protection of human and civil rights for homosexual persons was not just encouraged, but "mandated."[20]

The priests' report was thus an important step in ministry to the gay community. In practical terms it proposed the creation of a Board of Ministries that would assist parishes in providing welcome and services for gay and lesbian Catholics. The *BAR* responded to the document with a relatively positive account entitled, "Catholics Recognize Gay Love" subtitled, "However . . . No Sex!" The article found several of the reports assertions as "startling" or "surprising."[21]

Not as enthusiastic about the report were several members of the Task Force who saw the document as a step backward. In a news conference called for June 28, the anniversary of the Stonewall uprising in New York City, Task Force chair Kevin Gordon, along with members of Dignity San Francisco, Catholics for Human Dignity, and the Coalition for Human Rights, denounced the report as "theologically and pastorally inadequate and, therefore unacceptable . . . [the report] neither comes out of, nor speaks to, the real lives and loves of lesbian women and gay men." The report was therefore being "returned" to the archdiocese.[22]

The archdiocese responded quickly—two days later the Task Force on Gay and Lesbian Issues was dissolved for holding an "unauthorized" press conference—no notice had been given to the Commission on Social Justice. Though the immediate cause of the dissolution was the press conference, a letter to the *BAR* expressed what many people felt. "Well, well, well! Quinn and his obsequious cohorts have been scurrying frantically about for months trying to ferret out a 'reason' to pluck the Task Force thorn from their nettled flank. The 'reason' they finally came up with—the Task Force had the unmitigated gall to call a press conference without prior consultation with the Archdiocese—is patently and laughably specious. One wonders if they really thought they were fooling anybody."[23]

Gordon went on to establish his own group, the San Francisco Consultation on Homosexuality, Social Justice and Roman Catholic Theology, but he became increasingly bitter. In 1987, he continued to assert that the Catholic Church was a "conduit, if not the root cause, of oppression and violence" against gays and lesbians, but his days of influence within the Church in San Francisco had passed.[24]

---

20. Roberta Ward, "S.F. Senate of Priests Creates New Policy for Archdiocese," *SFM*, (June 2, 1983): 1, 12.

21. George Mendenhall, "Catholics Recognize Gay Love," *BAR*, (June 9, 1983): 1.

22. Don Lattin, "Gays Reply to Catholics: 'Unacceptable'," *SF Examiner*, (June 28, 1983): B4

23. C. B. Morrison, MD, "The Church and Press Conferences," *BAR*, (July 14, 1983).

24. Ray O'Loughlin, "Hearings Examine Links Between Church, Violence," *BAR*, (September 17, 1987): 4.

The AIDS Crisis

As Catholics debated the merits of the report, in late 1982, the gay community was gripped by a more compelling concern, indeed, a nightmare—the AIDS [Acquired Immune Deficiency Syndrome] crisis. The magnitude of the oncoming epidemic was not fully appreciated at first—many expressed disbelief in what some called the "gay cancer"—a deadly disease that affected primarily gay men. By the mid-1980s, more than thirty deaths each month in the city were attributed to AIDS, and the number of deaths was rising dramatically. Some religious saw the plague as divine retribution for the sin of homosexuality.

Quinn's response was measured and compassionate. He appointed a full-time AIDS minister, and a vacant convent in the Castro was converted into an AIDS hospice (by 1995, archdiocesan Catholic Charities would be the leading provider of housing for those affected by AIDS and HIV). In 1985, Most Holy Redeemer Parish in the Castro began offering an annual Forty Hours Devotion before the Blessed Sacrament to pray for those with AIDS and for their families, and to pray for an end to the scourge. Quinn regularly led the devotions. In addition, he was outspoken in condemning discrimination against people with AIDS. In June, 1986, Quinn issued a pastoral letter: "The AIDS Crisis: A Pastoral Response." He warned that the sickness must not be considered a sign of "divine retribution," and that the Christian response had to be one of compassion. "The Christian—the church—must not contribute to breaking the spirit of the sick and weakening their faith by harshness." Instead, the sickness should be regarded as "an invitation to enter into communion with the suffering of Christ and to contribute to the redemption of the world." Quinn concluded, "The church, then, as it passes through this new and virulent trial, must above all be a clear witness that the heart of Christ pierced on the Cross is the heart of Christ open in loving kindness to all who come to him."[25] The following year, with Quinn as president, the bishops of the California Catholic Conference issued a letter on AIDS entitled, "A Call to Compassion."

Quinn's stance on AIDS won him a grudging respect among some in the gay community. Several newspaper articles praised Quinn's personal ministry to those suffering from AIDS. A member of Dignity San Francisco noted that the AIDS crisis had given the Church and the gay community a common foe: "AIDS has given the Church and the gay community an opportunity to work together that didn't exist before." The Church's ministry to those suffering from AIDS raised a troubling reflection, however. "It's almost like the church is saying the only good gay Catholic is a dying gay Catholic."[26] A cynical cartoon that appeared in a local gay newspaper captured the dilemma. A young gay man is shown going to confession. The confessor says, "I'm sorry I can't help you. Come back when you are sick."

---

25. John R. Quinn, "The AIDS Crisis: A Pastoral Response," *America*, (June 28, 1986): 504–506.
26. Quoted in Don Lattin, "The Diplomat," *San Francisco Image*, (August 30, 1987): 18.

*Archbishop John R. Quinn
denounces discrimination against
people with AIDS. (Courtesy: Archives of
the Archdiocese of San Francisco)*

The Ratzinger Letter and the Papal Visit

In 1986 it was announced that Pope John Paul II would make an historic visit to San Francisco as part of his ten-day trip to the United States. The visit would place enormous strains on the relationship between gays and the Catholic Church in San Francisco.

Much of the ensuing discontent was instigated by the Vatican office of the Congregation for the Doctrine of Faith's letter to the world's bishops entitled, "On the Pastoral Care of Homosexual Persons," which became popularly known as the "Ratzinger Letter,"—named after Cardinal Joseph Ratzinger, prefect of the congregation. The letter, issued on October 30, 1986, was reported in the popular press as a vicious assault on gays and lesbians. Once again, the *Bay Area Reporter* captured the mood of the gay community with its front-page headline "Pope to Gays: 'Drop Dead.'"[27] While the whole letter was regarded as an insult, two passages were particularly galling. "Although the particular inclination of the homosexual is not a sin, it is a more or less strong tendency ordered toward an intrinsic moral evil, and thus the inclination itself must be seen as an objective disorder." And, "[When] homosexual activity is consequently condoned, or when civil legislation is introduced to protect behavior to which no one has any conceivable right, neither the church nor society at large should

27. "Pope to Gays: 'Drop Dead,'" *BAR*, (November 6, 1986).

be surprised when other distorted notions and practices gain ground, and irrational and violent reactions increase." The letter seemed to indicate that gays were themselves responsible for violence against gays, and that gays were responsible for the AIDS crisis. An editorial opinion provided by the National Gay and Lesbian Task Force condemned the letter in no uncertain terms, "Rather than preaching understanding and respect for other human beings, the church has unsheathed its sword and raised it against gay men and lesbians everywhere. The danger and terrorism represented by the Vatican's new statement cannot be understated: it will unleash the flames of ignorance and violence more effectively than a bomb ever could."[28]

For the next several months the *BAR's* letters to the editor ranted and fumed their outrage. Cartoons were printed ridiculing the pope. The *BAR* also ran an editorial condemning the letter; "Only a severely twisted soul could be taken in by the Vatican's recent letter on homosexuality as in any way a document for moral guidance."[29] Further, the editorial called for "an apology from the church" for this insult to the gay community.

The animosity engendered by the Ratzinger letter spilled over into protests against the papal visit. A petition circulated in the gay community with the simple message, "Pope, Stay Home!" Harassing civil suits were filed to prevent public moneys from being used for the visit and to void the contract to use Candlestick Park, claiming it violated the city's gay rights ordinance which forbade the city from contracting with organizations that discriminated on the basis of sexual orientation. Massive protests were planned, with the *BAR* suggesting this would be the "most difficult trip the pope may ever make."[30] As if to confirm growing Catholic fears of potentially embarrassing protests, the Sisters of Perpetual Indulgence registered with the city as the "Official San Francisco 1987 Papal Welcoming Committee."

The Archdiocese sought to counter the growing tensions. Archbishop Quinn published an interpretive reading of the Ratzinger letter, "Toward an Understanding of the Letter on the Pastoral Care of Homosexual Persons," published in *America* magazine on February 7, 1987. Quinn sought to soften the harshness of the letter by qualifying it. First, he noted, the letter was a technical document written for bishops, not the general public. Second, certain elements of the letter, especially its social commentary, did not require the same level of assent that had to be given to doctrinal formulations. Thus, the implication in the Ratzinger letter that gay demands were the source of violence against gays could be questioned. Third, Quinn even qualified the "central moral affirmation" of the letter: "It is only in the marital relationship that the use of the sexual faculty can be morally good. A person engaging in homosexual behavior therefore acts immorally." To which Quinn added, "Of course, in virtue of this principle, those who commit adultery or who engage in heterosexual behavior before marriage also act im-

---

28. "Editorial Opinion: Unleashing the Flames of Ignorance," *BAR*, (November 6, 1986): 6.
29. Ray O'Loughlin, "Editorial and Opinion: Twisted Thomas," *BAR*, (November 20, 1986): 6.
30. "Mass Dis-Appeal," *BAR*, (January 8, 1987): 4.

morally." Fourth, Quinn contended that too much focus had been placed on the negative aspects of the letter. He then listed six positive aspects of the letter, concluding, "[T]he document affirms the spiritual and human dignity of the homosexual *person* while placing a negative moral judgment on homosexual *acts* and a negative philosophical judgment on the homosexual *inclination* or orientation, which it clearly states is not a sin or moral evil."[31]

Quinn's article was a masterful reformulation of the Ratzinger letter. Psychologist Eugene Kennedy was in awe: "There's something artistic about the way he [Quinn] takes on difficult problems and works them out so they seem to disappear. After reading his article, you no longer feel like the Vatican letter is the end of the world."[32]

In June the archdiocese also opened negotiations with the gay community to try and avoid violence during the papal visit. After months of meetings under the direction of George Wesolek, the Archdiocesan Executive Director of the Peace and Justice Commission, "A Points of Unity for the Papal Visit" statement was issued. At a press conference held on September 8, several gay groups, most notably Dignity, joined the archdiocese in affirming the right to freedom of assembly and to freedom of speech, as well as committing themselves to non-violence and to promoting an "atmosphere of non-violence."[33]

The months of tough negotiations paid rich dividends during the papal visit. The promised massive demonstrations never materialized. Alternative events were celebrated and small protests—the largest numbering about 5,000—occurred throughout the city, but all protests remained orderly. Even the Sisters of Perpetual Indulgence protest went largely unnoticed. Instead huge crowds turned out to celebrate the Pope's visit. Many gay Catholics attended the papal events as well. Not everyone was enthusiastic. The week before the pope's visit, the *BAR* editorialized, "It is wrong for gay people to meet with the pope. It is an act which betrays our entire people. It is an act which gives power to a church which has for 19 centuries sought a systematic genocide of our people."[34]

Even so, the visit went remarkably well. During the planning stages it was suggested that the pope demonstrate his good will by visiting the Catholic AIDS hospice in Most Holy Redeemer Parish in the Castro. This could not be worked out so it was arranged that on the first night of the papal visit, Pope John Paul II would meet with AIDS patients, their families, friends, and caretakers at Mission Dolores. The event packed an enormous emotional wallop. In a particularly touching moment, the Pope embraced a young four-year old boy named Brendan O'Rourke who was suffering from AIDS. The congregation cheered. The event was captured in a memorable photograph and reprinted widely. Pope John Paul then delivered a powerful sermon, which

---

31. All quotes from John R. Quinn, "Toward an Understanding of the Letter on the Pastoral Care of Homosexual Persons," *America*, (February 7, 1987): 92–94.

32. Eugene Kennedy quoted in Don Lattin, "The Diplomat," 18.

33. Archives of the Archdiocese of San Francisco, Papal Visit—Gay Task Force File.

34. Ray O'Loughlin, "Editorial and Opinion: The Blood of Our Martyrs," *BAR*, (September 10, 1987): 6.

Pope John Paul II embraces a young boy who suffers from AIDS.

many interpreted as an olive branch to the gay community. The pope reminded the congregation of "the all embracing love of God . . . God loves you all, without distinction, without limit . . . He loves those of you who are sick, those who are suffering from AIDS and from AIDS-related complex. He loves the relatives and friends of the sick and those who care for them. He loves us all with an unconditional and everlasting love . . . he loves us in our human condition, with our weaknesses and our needs. Nothing else can explain the mystery of the cross . . . The love of Christ is more powerful than sin and death."[35] After a year of worries and fears, the papal visit ended peacefully. While many gay Catholics expressed ambivalence about the visit, others were deeply moved.

Even with the success of the papal visit, the difficulties between the Church and the gay community did not evaporate. Shortly after the visit, Quinn informed Dignity they could no longer celebrate mass in a Catholic church, so they moved to a Protestant church where they continued to celebrate mass. The issues of spousal benefits for "domestic partners," and the move for recognition of "same-sex marriages" soon caused growing public rancor. Nonetheless, during the decade 1977–1987, the Church in San Francisco had done a remarkable balancing act, one that entailed the need to be pastorally sensitive to gay Catholics, the need to speak out against violence against gays, and the need of remaining faithful to the Church's traditional teaching on marriage and sexuality.

---

35. Quoted in John Godges, "In the Face of AIDS, Pope John Paul II Brings Unconditional Love," *San Francisco Catholic* 3 (October 1987): 21.

Historicizing the People of God:
The Cushwa Center and the Vision
of its Founder

R. Scott Appleby

Founders leave their mark. Jay P. Dolan, the founder and first director of the Cushwa Center for the Study of American Catholicism at the University of Notre Dame, is by turns colorful, kind, playful, warm, aloof, engaged, retiring, irrepressible. His love for Notre Dame and the Catholic Church renewed by Vatican II shone through his penetrating criticisms of both institutions when they failed to live up to their own lofty ideals. Evoking nothing so much as a charming, slightly roguish, cigar-chomping, latter-day Irish pol who camouflages his status as the smartest kid in the class with a colloquial delivery and easygoing manner, Dolan the administrator and academic leader was, above all else, a shrewd and relentless advocate for the rigorous historical study of American Catholicism. No one worked harder in the seventies and eighties to lift the field to respectability in the larger secular academic world. When I succeeded him as director of the Cushwa Center in 1993, I found, unsurprisingly, that I had inherited a vital, thriving operation built on solid scholarly and financial foundations.

By that time, seventeen years after the University, at Dolan's urging, had officially established a Center for the Study of American Catholicism in the Fall of 1976, and twelve years after the Charles and Margaret Hall Cushwa family of Youngstown, Ohio had endowed it in 1981, the Cushwa Center was the pre-eminent site of the historical and interdisciplinary study of the Roman Catholic community in the United States. A nationally recognized resource for researchers who visited Notre Dame to consult its impressive collection of Catholic Americana, the Cushwa Center was also known for the regional seminar and national conferences it sponsored; the research and publication projects conceived by the director and his colleagues at Notre Dame and across the country; its financial support, through travel and dissertation grants, of scholars undertaking research on multiple dimensions of Catholic life and thought; and, not least, the *American Catholic Studies Newsletter,* which reported on new trends and publications in the field, the status of archive collections, and significant new research in progress.[1]

As other essays in this issue attest, Dolan the historian was a pioneer. To the field, or sub-field, of American Catholic history he applied the insights and methods of the new social history, choosing to study laity rather than clergy, the people in the parish rather than the bishops in their chanceries. The Immigrant Church was Dolan's métier; if clergy and religious warranted primary consideration, as they did in *Catholic Revivalism*, he zeroed in on the nexus where "the official church" encountered, shaped and was shaped by the "people of God." Dolan situated himself squarely within the new model of church proclaimed by Vatican II, which he saw as a much-needed revision of "the more traditional view of the church as a hierarchical institution in which the pope and his clergy reigned like monarchs." In typically straightforward, almost blunt language, Dolan defined his historical project as a direct response to the new ecclesiology. "One obvious effect of this change is the desire to write a new history of Roman Catholicism," he explained in the preface to his landmark survey, *The American Catholic Experience*. "A new understanding of the church demands a new history of Roman Catholicism."[2]

Beyond his own scholarship Dolan pursued the writing of this new history through the agendas he and others set for the Cushwa Center. The close identification with the spirit of the council meant, among other things, that Catholic scholars, like the church itself, must abandon a fortress mentality and the religio-cultural enclaves within which intellectual enquiry had been confined for generations. The closed professional guild was to be supplanted by a new configuration remaining to be specified, but certainly informed by "ecumenical," "interdisciplinary," and "secular" concerns and methods. Indeed, the idea for what became the Cushwa Center originated while Dolan was a Fellow at the Shelby Cullom Davis Center for Historical Studies at Princeton University in 1973–74. Significantly, he took that secular, strictly academic and research-oriented enterprise as a model for the initiative he would inspire at Notre Dame.

During my term as director of the Cushwa Center we have spoken frequently of the need and desire to integrate the study of Catholicism with the mainstream of American social and cultural history. This was Jay's vision all along, of course, and he built the Cushwa Center with it in mind. Thus, he rooted the Center in an academic department at Notre Dame (History), deftly avoiding affiliation with the institutional church or with primarily pastoral initiatives at Notre Dame such as the Institute for Pastoral and Social Ministry (later the Institute for Church Life). This decision may seem obvious today, but at the time there were pressures on the new, resource-thin Center to ensure its survival through formal association with another center or program already en-

---

1. Jeffrey M. Burns, "In Service of American Catholic Studies: The Charles and Margaret Hall Cushwa Center for the Study of American Catholicism," *U.S. Catholic Historian* 3 (1983): 20–34.

2. Jay. P. Dolan, *The American Catholic Experience: A History from Colonial Times to the Present* (Garden City, N.Y.: Doubleday, 1985), 10.

trenched within the University. To his credit, Dolan resisted the temptation. This bit of Dolanesque foresight enabled Cushwa gradually to build its reputation and autonomy as an academic center, thereby ultimately strengthening its capacity to serve the church on its own terms and within its own disciplinary boundaries. And serve the church it did, initially through a series of historical projects devoted to developing a deeper and more sophisticated historical understanding of American Catholic parishes and popular religion.

The first of these historical studies of the parish unfolded in conjunction with the Notre Dame Study of Catholic Parish Life. The Cushwa Center commissioned six historians to produce regionally specific social histories of the American parish. In keeping with conciliar Catholicism's focus on the local church, the essays, published in two volumes under the title, *The American Catholic Parish: A History from 1850 to the Present* (New York: Paulist Press, 1987), explored lay involvement and leadership in the parish, the religious practices of the people, the relationship between ethnicity and parish affiliation, and parochial education. In a subsequent project, building on the findings reported in the regional histories, a team of three historians analyzed the changing roles of priests, laity, and women religious in the parish from 1930 to 1985; their monograph-length essays were published by Crossroad/Continuum in 1989 under the title *Transforming Parish Ministry.* (Patricia Byrne's splendid account of the rapid evolution of the self-understanding, religious identity, and apostolic mission of women religious remains a standard work in the field.) In planning and carrying out these research projects the Cushwa Center typically took full advantage of Notre Dame's collection of parish histories and extensive materials in the University's archives.

Taken alone, the parish studies, however rich and nuanced, could not significantly advance the study of American Catholicism beyond the confines of the pre-conciliar "closed guild" model. Dolan's vision of the Cushwa Center as a national Catholic and ecumenical research center in dialogue with the American academic mainstream therefore dictated a multiple-track educational and research strategy. Thus, alongside the studies of the parish and popular religious life among Catholics, the Cushwa Center sponsored periodic national conferences designed to enlarge the scope of the field by inviting contributions from a broad range of historians, theologians and sociologists across the country.

Some of these conferences addressed innovative methodological and topical approaches to the study of American Catholicism drawn from the new ethnic studies and social history ("Reinterpretations of American Catholic History," 1974) or from the work of historians of race, gender, and culture ("The Cultures of American Catholicism," 1985). Others explored the comparative experience of Catholics, Lutherans, and Dutch Calvinists in the United States ("Perspectives on American Catholicism," 1982) or the European contexts and cultural backgrounds of U.S. Catholicism ("Ireland and the United States: The Transatlantic Connection, 1800–1980" [1987] and "History of Christianity" [1992]). The numbers in attendance at these conferences, as well as the quality of the papers presented, increased dramatically over the years as the Cushwa Center earned the national reputation it now enjoys.

In their thematic scope and inclusive spirit, the major conferences sponsored by the Cushwa Center in the years following Dolan's retirement as director built upon and extended this legacy of interaction with a diverse range of scholars. "Engendering American Catholicism," a series of working group sessions and seminar discussions held in 1995, was designed to attract a new generation of cultural and social historians to the field and particularly to the study of Catholic women and the complex relationships between the genders—relationships that were shaped in large part by theological, ecclesial, and psychological dynamics operating during the period in question. "Catholicism in Twentieth-Century America," held at Notre Dame in March 2000, was the culminating conference of a major research project dedicated to original research exploring the diverse public presences of Catholics in the United States; the varied interactions between Catholics and other Americans in the workplace, the academy, labor unions, and the like; and the internal ethnic, gender, and cultural diversity of the Catholic community.

Seminar, lecture and publications series developed by Dolan during the formative years of the Cushwa Center replicated this pattern of complementary but distinct approaches to the study of American Catholicism. The American Catholic Studies Seminars, held three or four times a year at Notre Dame, were devoted primarily to discussions of work in progress by graduate students and newly minted Ph.D.'s. Here the focus was on honing one's craft and polishing one's arguments before a small audience of faculty and students conversant with the historical literature on Catholicism in the United States; the papers were revised following the seminar discussion and made available to a larger public through a Working Paper Series. The Annual Hibernian Lecture, sponsored by the Ancient Order of Hibernians, was likewise narrowly focused, on the experience of Irish and Irish American Catholics (or, occasionally, of Ulster Protestants as well).

Dolan established two successful Notre Dame Press publication series corresponding to these areas of expertise. Notre Dame Studies in American Catholicism eventually came to include fourteen titles, several of which continue to exercise influence in the field (e.g., Ann Taves, *The Household of Faith: Roman Catholic Devotions in Mid-Nineteenth Century America*; William M. Halsey, *The Survival of American Innocence: Catholicism in an Era of Disillusionment, 1920–1940*). The Irish in America Series has produced four volumes, the most recent of which is *'Inventing Irish America:' Generation, Class, and Ethnic Identity in a New England City, 1880–1928*, Timothy Meagher's excellent study of the Irish American community of Worcester, Massachusetts.

Meanwhile, Dolan broadened the scope and appeal of the Cushwa Center by establishing a lecture series on religion and public life; by sponsoring colloquia on the history of women religious and American Catholics and the Holy Land; and by chairing a consultation on the study of Hispanic Catholicism. The Seminar in American

Religion quickly became the Center's most popular and well-known regular event. Held each semester at Notre Dame, the Saturday morning seminar is devoted to a vigorous critical discussion of a recent and influential book in American religion. The author of the book is not on trial, exactly, but it is perhaps worth noting that Martin E. Marty, a longtime friend of the Cushwa Center and the doctoral mentor of its two directors, still refers, in his genial manner, to the discussion of *The Irony of It All,* the first volume in his monumental history of modern American religion, as "Fricaseed Marty." Two commentators initiate the two-hour-plus seminar discussion; participants include historians, sociologists, and theologians from colleges and universities in the upper Midwest. Noted authors who have survived and even enjoyed the experience include Robert Orsi, Jan Shipps, Robert Wuthnow, Catherine Brekus, Nathan Hatch, Joel Carpenter, James Turner, George Marsden, Jon Butler, Phil Gleason, and John McGreevy.

The cumulative impact of these varied initiatives strongly suggests that the Dolan years were marked by inclusiveness, a celebration of pluralism in method and subject, and a commitment to telling the stories of all the multi-ethnic, multi-cultural "people of God." One finds confirmation of this argument in the final major project administered, co-conceptualized, and co-edited by Dolan, the series of conferences and correspondences that led to the publication of the three volumes of historical essays examining and analyzing the experiences of "Hispanic Catholics" in the United States.[3] As usual, Dolan had the Cushwa Center slightly ahead of the curve; the series, while receiving criticism from some quarters for omitting or slighting certain topics, was a landmark study of a topic whose time had clearly come. (The comments of one reviewer were typical; he confirmed the editors' hopes that the series represented "a new plateau" and "a significant step forward in the elaboration of a United States Catholic church history that gives the remarkable Hispanic presence the recognition it rightly deserves.") In planning this important project and bringing it to fruition the "pragmatic Irish pol" exhibited characteristic shrewdness in surrounding himself with experts in a field of study that few non-Latina/o scholars had mastered.

* * *

Little of this research, writing and conferencing could have been accomplished without the benefit of Dolan's considerable political, administrative and fund-raising skills. The Dolan "style" combined common sense, practical insight into human nature, and a detailed knowledge not only of the historical literature on American Catholicism and American religion as a whole, but of the broader horizons of Ameri-

---

3. Jay P. Dolan and Gilberto M. Hinojosa, eds., *Mexican Americans and the Catholic Church, 1900–1965* (Notre Dame, University of Notre Dame Press, 1994); Jay P. Dolan and Jaime R. Vidal, eds., *Puerto Rican and Cuban Catholics in the U.S., 1900–1965* (Notre Dame, University of Notre Dame Press, 1994); Jay P. Dolan and Allan Figueroa Deck, S.J., eds., *Hispanic Catholic Culture in the U.S.: Issues and Concerns* (Notre Dame, University of Notre Dame Press, 1994).

can society and culture. In a testimonial letter addressed to Dolan upon the occasion of his retirement from the Cushwa Center directorship, Jeanne Knoerle, for many years program officer at the Lilly Endowment, recalled:

> I always knew when you walked in the door of the Endowment with that casual, innocent look, wanting "just to talk," that we would be *had* before you left. The conversation would begin quietly with a few offhand comments, then the stakes would increase as you carefully added a piece here and a piece there, embroidering the original suggestions from the basketful of ideas you had hidden under that innocent casualness. And before long, there it was, the fully developed, artfully prepared proposal that was the real reason you had come. And we were goners . . . But I am glad you came. And I'm glad we had the intelligence (and the money) to respond to your good ideas. Those visits produced many excellent projects which made unique and important contributions to the history of American Catholicism.

In addition to developing strong relationships with foundation officers and colleagues in universities across the nation, Jay had great respect and affection for the Cushwas, keeping in regular contact with Mrs. Margaret Hall Cushwa, her son Charles, and other family members. William and Anna Jean Cushwa, the son and daughter-in-law of the original benefactors and, like them, lay leaders of the Roman Catholic community of Ohio, have recently extended the family's remarkable support of the study of American Catholicism at Notre Dame by generously providing for the endowment of the director's position. This gift will enable the Cushwa Center to remain a national and international center of excellence in the study of Roman Catholicism.

The two great accomplishments of Jay Dolan's career—his own influential scholarship and his long and productive tenure as founding director of the Cushwa Center—constitute a remarkable gift to historians of American Catholicism, American religion and American society in general. As a result of Dolan's vision and ambition, the University of Notre Dame came closer to achieving its aspiration to become a first-rate national Catholic research university. Not least, the "people of God"—that vision of the universal church that Dolan internalized and helped others to understand and appreciate—had a powerful advocate in a social historian whose greatest legacy is his commitment, institutionalized in the Cushwa Center, to ensure that no perspective or voice be excluded from the telling and memorializing of "the American Catholic experience."

Locating Jay P. Dolan

Martin E. Marty

Authors of *Festschriften* characteristically attempt to locate those they honor, in place and in time.

Locating Jay Dolan in place, literally, is an easy task. His whole academic career found him at the University of Notre Dame du Lac, where he has served in a spirit of institutional loyalty and with admirable energy and creativity. Except when he has done research on sabbaticals at locations in Ireland or when he has been attending or presenting at gatherings of fellow historians, his address, his location, has been near the Golden Dome in South Bend, Indiana.

Locating, of course, has a figurative dimension. Sometimes the act of locating places one in hierarchies or on ladders of rankings. Where do we "place" Professor Dolan among those of his profession? Answers to such a question preoccupy those who celebrate at *Festschrift* time.

Nothing so idle speaking of him or anyone else as "Number One" or "Number Two" will be intellectually satisfying. There are no clear objective criteria for such a ratings game. Suffice it to say that in any evaluation of the generation that furthered the study of American Catholic history toward the turn of the millennium, Dolan has been a leader recognized across the map of the profession and beyond it. His writing, his teaching, his service as president of the two main associations in our craft, and his pioneering work at the Cushwa Center poised him well for his central role. And the extent and substance of that already mentioned writing positions him to be reckoned with for some time to come.

"For some time to come . . . ." Locating historians in time, and thus in history, is somewhat more difficult. Where does the generation in which he was a leader "fit" in respect to those that preceded him in this vocation? How will he and his generation be regarded as the new generation(s) take(s) its place?

In one sense, locating historians, including and maybe especially, historians who deal with religious themes, is difficult because we historians are most conscious of transience. We are in the business of recording the transient on the way to being recognized as having been embodiments and exemplars of the transient.

It may be that a young philosopher on the way up conceives of himself as a candidate for permanence, for a place in the pantheon as a possessor and propagator of new and profound ideas. A budding theologian may picture herself as representing a dream of entering the Theological Hall of Fame. There is no Cooperstown for church-and-religious historians, if there is for what we call secular historians. Anyone who goes to graduate school and chooses history, especially religious history, as a way of gaining immortality or enduring influence, should not have been accepted into the program. Living with such aspirations and illusions is a sign that the candidate has not read widely or deeply in the archives or libraries, has not browsed in the bookstores.

Not that historians' names are, to use John Keats's fluid image for the flowing, "writ in water." In Great Books courses people read Herodotus and Thucydides and Gibbon—and who else? In the religious equivalent of Great Books courses some might read the author of Luke-Acts—let's at least start out pretentiously by claiming him for the profession—and Eusebius. (Augustine was a philosopher of history, so we cannot claim him).

After Eusebius? From there on the field belongs to specialists, readers of chronicles, annals, archival materials, or long-ago published books that, however "great" they were—and many were great—do not become Great Books. In the nature of the case, no matter what their art and science demonstrate, they get located with the era about which they wrote or in which they lived, which means they are passing.

When I first taught American Catholic history to well-read graduate students, be they Catholic, American, religious by background, or not, I could not assume that any of them except those who brought master's degrees in Catholic historical studies, had heard of, to say nothing of having read, the landmarkers and buoy-placers of the longer past, John Gilmary Shea and Peter Guilday. Some of them had read John Tracy Ellis, who was still in his prime. (Until his death year whenever I wrote him I would get back a postcard to the effect that as long as the Holy Spirit gave him breath, he would be writing church history.) If I were to carve a sandstone Mount Rushmore of American Catholic historians, those three might be the first three heads represented. I leave to the readers the game of nominating a fourth, and thus coming close to playing the "Who's Number One?" game that verges on being pointless and fruitless.

Jay Dolan was aware of that as he entered the profession and has to be aware of it as he reaches seniority. His shelves like mine are full of journal articles and books on "the new history," of writings by those in generations that follow, that often suggest and sometimes demonstrate promising departures, new discoveries, and new perspectives. Dolan, if he was possessed of nothing else, owns and works with perspective, so he can both look with hope to the new aspirants even as he casts a wry if weary Irish eye or forms a veteran's smile at the notion that anything can be all *that* new and displacing in what is coming up among newer historians.

Mentioning that neither Shea or Guilday or Ellis or anyone in the Dolan generation will have influence beyond the profession, or even beyond specialists within the profession, is not insulting to any of the people mentioned here, including and especially

Dolan. We get clues to that from a consistent *sotto voce* theme, a minor-key *cantus firmus* under all his reflective writings. It sings the sad lay that American Catholics are not, as a group, highly curious about their history. He must look, as I do, at the popular and academic magazines and journals aimed at general publics and see how almost every issue will deal with some aspect of Jewish history. Jews buy books, care about their identity and prospects as a people, and write and review and buy and read books, as Catholics do not.

Sometimes as I reread him in preparation for this celebration I thought of the Catholic historian related to the Catholic people making history, in the mode of Dylan Thomas writing poetry about love but going unnoticed, apparently unneeded and unheeded, by lovers: in the poet's "craft or sullen art/Exercised . . . when lovers lie abed," he wrote "for the common wages/Of their most secret heart." Yet, he concludes, they "pay no praise or wages/Nor heed my craft or art."[1]

Thomas did not stop writing poetry because there was not a big lovers' market. Neither did Dolan and his professional kin and kith stop writing because Catholics in the main do not read Catholic history. Emphatically: Dolan is not a whiner, a whinger, a complainer. He is a doer. First, like all of us, he believes that historical writing has intrinsic value. Second, he shows that he knows, with Theodor Adorno, that most of history is about suffering people. That is true of more members than not of the immigrant church about which he has written so well. More Adorno: *not* ever to tell the story is therefore to dishonor the suffering, the sufferers, and thus the human.

More, Dolan knows, with G. J. Renier, a Dutch historian who influenced numbers of us at mid-century, that the historian writes for when people "stop to think." Most of us historians don't read, can't read, most of what our colleagues publish. Most Catholic historians cannot begin to read all that their fellow historians of Catholicism publish. Whoever has read the bibliographies that issued from the Cushwa Center when under the directorship of Jay Dolan and then R. Scott Appleby, would despair of catching up or keeping up on even a fragment of it. But, as Renier contended, when a person, a community or association of nation, must "stop to think," they can draw upon what the historians have presented custodially in quiet through the generations.

Dolan's intention, and the direction of his work, is pointed to Catholics who "stop to think" about their identity, and who will find it by learning more of where they come from and what they inherit. The parallel intention in his work has been to help other Americans clarify their own identity, which is done in the face of the "other." And the other, for three-fourths of them for a century and for a larger percentage from 1607 to the twentieth century, has been the Catholic people.

The Catholic people. Dolan, more than his predecessors, has been the historian not of the hierarchy, the religious orders, the institutional leadership—though they, too are "Catholic people," and one cannot tell the people's story without them—but of the

---

1. "In My Craft or Sullen Art," reprinted in Oscar Williams, ed., *The Mentor Book of Major British Poets* (New York: The New American Library, 1963), p. 560

people. He will be measured for his success or failure in that respect. I see mainly success, and those who follow him in the writing of "social history" readily pay regard to him for his work in this field, work that anticipates, often inspires, and regularly influences their refinements and particular inquiries. The question at *Festschrift* time is: *how* has he conceived and written about the Catholic people?

Had Dolan been writing, and did he still write, in a triumphalist spirit, he would have planned obsolescence into the work. Unlike predecessors in the Guilday and Ellis generations, he had the advantage of having his formation take place after the Second Vatican Council. Sometimes criticized for making too much of the Council as watershed or turning-point, especially by those who do not have a personal adult living memory of the church before it, he knew that overstating the case for Catholicism in American history would represent bad taste, if not foolishness. Tooting the trumpets was no longer necessary when he began writing.

Secondly, he has not been telling the story as some predecessors and non-historian apologists within Catholicism have been doing, as determined by the Catholic presence in a hostile, which means Protestant environment. Again, one cannot tell the story without accounting for the siege mentality of Protestants of the past having an effect on the Catholic outlook—for the dominating spirit that both forced Catholics into what used to be called "the Catholic ghetto" and found them accepting its terms for a long time. But he has not made *The Protestant Crusade*, to use Ray Billington's apt name for the nativist attacks, the definer. Dolan's story has always been more what Catholics have been doing, not what has been done to them.

Even more important than those two is a third: he has no Oedipal case against the Church of the past, as many liberated, late-twentieth century Catholic writers, again, not most of them historians, have been developing. If as an historian he has to be a hanging judge, a maker of judgments, he has shown an ability that many recent writers have not. He judges people in the context of the possibilities of their own time, not applying standards that developed among those lucky enough to have been born later. Thus, people who lived pre-Abolition, pre-Woman Suffrage, pre-liberation, pre-civil rights movement, pre-Vatican II do not get slashed or smashed or hanged. Dealing with them has not been a main theme, as it is for so many ex-Catholics, writers more critical than the militants in *The Protestant Crusade* ever were.

This does not mean that as he tells his story he gives either triumphalist Catholics nor their antagonist Crusaders a free ride. Rather, he lets that story be his guide. Few compliments come higher than this one: he has confidence in his story, in the telling of it, and of reader response, be it Catholic or not. This has meant that the story of hierarchs, even the self-important, is told fairly as part of the larger story, not as an excuse to trash them. This means that members of religious orders and priests come on or off stage as members of "the Catholic people" and not as castes or breeds apart, candidates for either apotheosis or stigmatization.

So, *how* did he, does he approach the history of the Catholic people?

First, by changing emphasis from what had gone before. I hope it will not be seen as gauche for me to quote myself, from the Foreword to his first book. Doing so will help me and others make assessments now further along in Dolan's career. After Shea, I wrote, "the volumes on the American Catholic past are preponderantly ecclesiastical in tone. They concentrate on the people who rose to positions of leadership or on institutions in apparent isolation from their environments." Then followed a rough statistical reckoning:

"Whoever scans . . . extensive bibliographies such as John Tracy Ellis's *A Guide to American Catholic History* [in its first, unrevised, more slight edition, conscience impels me to note] will find chiefly the following topics: diocesan and sectional history (203 items); biographies, correspondence, and memoirs of Catholic dignitaries and leaders (301 items); religious communities (70 items); education—chiefly institutional (64 items)."

We did find "some more promising books in the older Ellis bibliography," promising for those who like Dolan were to write on "the people." There were 22 parish histories, "some of them attentive to the people's experience and, best of all, over ninety books on colonization, journalism, law, missions, nationalism, nativism, social studies, wars, and the like." But those who studied these "will often be disappointed . . . by the official tone or institutional awe that marks much of it." My paragraph ended with a notice that Ellis himself had made the move of seeing Catholicism "in the context of American political history," new for his generation though, alas, disdained by many social history exclusivists.[2]

So Dolan came on the scene in the company of those in a generation of types as "social historians." Line one of the Foreword quoted British Marxist historian E. J. Hobsbawm, "It is a good moment to be a social historian;" and "social history is at present in fashion," and that "writing the history of society" is a valid enterprise."[3] Dolan would join that enterprise.

He has to be seen as a pioneer in that field, and as one who has encouraged the development of and publicity for hundreds of dissertations and articles in that genre, especially from the years of his Cushwa directorship. He must be bemused by those who speak, a quarter of a century later, of their social history enterprise as "new," for example, in "the new history." I am amused to read breathless claims for the novelty of the new. Most historians date this approach or see its consolidation and proposals for more of it with the birth of the *Annales* journal and school in France. It may be "new" to those who have not read the historians in that tradition since its founding, which was in 1928. So it is precisely as old as I am, I who enjoy being part of the discovery of "the new social history."

There are departures and refinements, of course, and Dolan would be the first to celebrate them. Some of these have to do with scale. I recall world-historian William McNeill once describing how different historians find different vocations. He had found himself called to be what I would call a big-picture, big-scale historian, who

---

2. Foreword to Jay P. Dolan, *The Immigrant Church: New York's Irish and German Catholics, 1815–1865*. (Baltimore: Johns Hopkins University Press, 1975), x, xi.

3. Ibid., ix.

would write on topics as vast as *The Rise of the West*. Of course, he got his credentials from having written about the Balkan potato famines. But later he would use a vast canvas to write about, say, disease and history anywhere, any time.

Dolan's picture is not on the scale of McNeill's; his canvas is not so vast. Yet he has, in the main, not written monographs of an extremely close up character. His work on the immigrant church covers only (only!) a fifty-year period. His writing on revivalism has to do with a nineteenth century phenomenon. Both of them, though they offer provocative remarks pointing to synthesis, were Dolan's analogues to McNeill's potato famine writing. They dealt with only a few locations, were close-ups of only a few parishes in a few cities or counties. From them we get confidence to follow Dolan as he makes some generalizations in his *The American Catholic Experience*. But that book and his way of approaching others, including especially those he edited on the parish enterprise, suggest that his calling has been something like McNeill's: to venture with the bigger picture.

The close-up, nitty-gritty, archive-dust breathers, on whom other historians, certainly all generalizers, must depend, can point out that in his big book, Dolan as social historian does little close-up work. He cites that of others. His footnotes are, in effect, a bibliography citing what others had done by the date of publication, 1985. He therefore pays due respect to their genre and achievement while necessarily depending upon these as he builds is own figurative scaffolding for his real stories.

How does he address "the people's history?" Titles of two of his authored books and several of his edited ones help us isolate themes. I also read bibliographies of his own essays and articles and reviews, though, of course I did not read or reread all of them. What do we find? A rough count finds 13 titles matching the themes of *The Immigrant Church*, 12 those of *The American Catholic Experience,* (titles that conjoin "American" and "Catholic" chiefly). Four of them have "parish" or its analogues in their title, but articles on education and the like accent the parish, as he does in several edited volumes. Only three dealt explicitly with "Catholic Revivalism," but interest in it and evidences of his reading suffuse many of his other essays.

This is not the place to go into detail on other categories, including the writing of Catholic history, which came up directly in six of the published essays and colors his synthetic works. But there was only one about priests; only a couple on Protestantism; there were a few ventures into discussing race, and the like. But getting the Catholic people here, seeing them whipped up and gathered in, and finding them where they found community and identity, in the parish, are his themes.

How obvious, one might say; yet, how underdeveloped before his generation— Shea's writing, among the majors, apart. Yet not obvious enough to fill the bibliographical listings. There are many reasons for that, including the absence of developed techniques; the lack of a premium upon it or curiosity about it; the situation of archival access or the neglect of "people's history" in archives, given the auspices and preoccupations of most archive-holders; the fact that the role of women (other than religious) in American Catholic history and, with it, topics dealing with children, healing, domesticity, and the like were not prized. These lacks do not mean that those before

Dolan's generation were ignorant or prejudiced or whatever else judgmental later generations would like to pin on them. It means that they were doing different things, satisfying curiosities other than those we tend now to pursue. It also means that they were responsible to their superiors, the institutions and orders that housed them, in ways that university-based academics do not have to be or even always want to be.

In a time when some question whether meta-narratives can exist, be discerned, diagnosed, celebrated, or expounded; whether they can form backdrops to a story, we find Dolan assuming the value of a Catholic presence in American life, but not neglecting what is on this side of meta-narratives: stories of people who may not naturally hook up with others and with the stories of others. But he never joined the company of those who deserted narrative itself. I have not questioned him on this, but I picture him seeing the beginnings of the creation of new not-meta but still skeined-together stories. When we tell stories we may not be philosophers, but something impels us to certain topics and not others. As I read the histories of those who determine to write "multi-culturalist" sub-narratives, I find their topic choices progressively predictable. It does not take long to find the George Washingtons and Jonathan Edwardses, the Cardinal Gibbonses and Mary Baker Eddys replaced or complemented by just as predictable a set of counter-mainstream, once-marginal characters who have moved to the center: early feminists, African-Americans, "differently gendered" heroines and heroes, and the like. Historians like Dolan, by accenting "the people's history" anticipate the multi-cultural side but also find coherences where some of the newer particularists who are wary of narrative claim not to.

The social historians, the new historians, and those who recover narrative, Dolan anticipating them at their best, can be faulted and have been faulted for some of their omissions. Thus it is regularly pointed out that one of the grand schemas of religious history in the West, the narrative of theological development, rarely appears on Dolan's pages. True. But there are several good reasons for this. Not all historians are called to be intellectual historians, and social historians need not have theological and philosophical history as sub-specialties. Second, most of the periods about which Dolan has written produced little theology worth writing about. After one says that until Vatican II American Catholic theology was largely imported from Europe; was of late-scholastic sorts that quickened little interest; was under the protective custodianship of seminary faculties; was unknown except in highly distilled (e.g., "Baltimore Catechism" versions) among the laity, one can find reason not to fault Dolan and company on this score.

Still, ideas have consequences, and when Dolan takes up the ideas behind the controversy, for example, over religious freedom up to and through the Council, he has to be the historian of ideas, and treats them fairly. He at least describes what the grand figures from John Carroll through Orestes Brownson and Isaac Hecker and Walter Elliott proposed and how they conceived Catholicism in America.

To have done more would have been to misrepresent the actual place of formal theology among the lay millions in any period, at least until the Council. Until then,

Dolan is right, Tridentine Catholicism prevailed, and was passed on by those who love the rote, the canonical, the juridical, the codified.

Edmund Husserl has his phenomenologists being sophisticatedly naïve. They encounter a new landscape, for example, an island. Lacking a map or knowledge as to whether it had ever been mapped, they are especially attentive. Parking their presuppositions at the home port, they "see" the obvious that they might overlook.

So the grand strophes of Dolan's social history are the overlooked obvious.

The Immigrant Church. Of course, *every* historian wrote about an immigrant church, including those who dealt with Catholicism and Native Americans—thanks to the fact the missioners were immigrant. Certainly, every historian of American Catholicism dealing with the two centuries following 1634 dealt with an immigrant church. But it was from the 1830s through 1924, with its immigration restriction, and 1960, the election of John F. Kennedy, and other symbolic dates, that immigration was conceived in a particular way.

This can be seen from reflection on the familiar story of Franklin Delano Roosevelt's salutation in an address to the anti-immigrant, anti-outsider, Daughters of the American Revolution: "Fellow immigrants. . . ." Now we see their story as the story of immigrants, but not in the way the Catholics who came later (like the Lutherans from the Continent, and their counterparts) remained immigrants, with all the rites and privileges and wrongs attendant thereto. Dolan, using the immigrant motif, got very close to the people.

Husserl's phenomenologist would be pleased with us that we have noticed that Catholic people migrated to these shores. But then comes another obvious question: how gather them, rally, them, build morale, swell numbers, assure a future? Of course, again, many had told stories of moves in these directions. These were moves congruent with missionary activity in times past. But Dolan asked further questions: were there any extraordinary, less precedented, not imported approaches? Yes, says *Catholic Revivalism*. There were techniques to be borrowed from evangelical Protestants, or readings of situations similar to theirs. So Dolan has told the story of religious orders and lay congregations of the faithful who did what Protestants had learned, were still learning to do: revive, quicken, awaken, corral, and vivify new converts—usually immigrants off the boat who did not come with much spiritual resource, or had lost it.

It is hard to look at broad swaths of Catholic enterprise uninformed by what Dolan calls "revivalism," and it makes up part of the heritage and identity of today's Catholics, even though they might run from the term Dolan uses.

The third of his grand themes, not developed at book-length in his own authorial corpus, but strong in his editorial work: the parish. Once more, Husserl's naïvely sophisticated explorer would find it obvious that you might tell the story of American Catholicism through its most visible institution, the one closest to the people: the parish. Yet few historians had done much with it; most of them wrote chronicles of particular parishes in isolation and without bringing much by way of conceptual framework.

In the period when social historians looked for a place to do snapshots, issue stop-action commands, or find close-ups, the parish was the place for immigrants and the revived and everyone else self-named Catholic. Dolan participated in major efforts to find conceptuals, methods, locations, and impetuses from his Cushwa post and down the road from another Hoosier place, the sponsoring Lilly Endowment. So he edited several volumes on the Catholic parish, from the people's angle, so much as possible.

When Dolan does his ruing about the analogs to the poets who care not for Dylan Thomas's poems, the Catholics who do not care for or about American Catholic history, he does suggest a variety of reasons for quickening interest. Many of these have to do with Catholic identity. So long as it could be taken for granted there was very little curiosity about this. One just "found" it or owned it unreflectively. But today, with the weakening of denominations, parishes, structures, including in the case of Catholics; with Tridentine Catholicism having waned; with the exposure of Catholics to American life in scenes as intimate as the intermarriaged bedroom to the pluralist academy and market, the question of identity is important, and Dolan believes that telling and reading stories will be informing and empowering tasks.

Dolan's colleague Philip Gleason has written perceptively on the dangers of making too much of identity, as in "identity fad." But much of what he criticizes or finds short-sighted is not what Dolan has in his sights. At any rate, he has reason to make a new case for the search for communal identity in a time of general erosion of community boundaries and dissipation of traditions.

For Dolan, Catholicism is not something Platonic, ethereal, or merely the subject for cultural historians. In his first book he chanced to use a word that Father John Courtney Murray used to bring out the scandal of Catholic particularity in America awash in the seas of pluralism. The Church also is not gaseous, individualized, as the construct of Spirituality today turned out to be. No, the word is, it is a "thing." It is palpable, scandalous (which means you can trip over it, say etymologists), blocking the way, or providing ground to stand on.

The image Dolan uses for this "tangibilification" of God's work—the word is borrowed from Father Divine—is the concrete location of the local parish, the building itself. "The church the immigrant knew was not an abstract entity," Dolan writes (*The Immigrant Church*, 4). "It was localized and represented in the neighborhood parish church. Built of wood or stone, it occupied space in the neighborhood; people could see it, touch it, and enter inside it to pray or simply get out of the cold." As with the building, so with the Church as thing, embodiment, entity, in all Dolan's work. He has never romanticized the immigrant, revived, parish church. "Conflict in the Church" was an early chapter title and remains a theme. But if not romantic or nostalgic, Dolan is convicted, sure that if later generations get in touch with that which can be touched, they will have no ways to discover or fabricate the kind of identity social groups need to survive and prosper.

We would not read him on this subject were he an overt apologist, a public relations agent, a booster, or a nag. We read him, and I hope we will read him for decades to come, because he "touches" the people, their lives, and our hearts with their story, his story.

Locating him in our modest discipline, against the background of an often unheeding company, and reminding ourselves of the transience that comes to our work in the face of succeeding generations, was not damning with faint praise. For what he has done for the moment, his generation and its immediate successors, and all of us informed and, yes, often inspired by his work, we can remove all hints of faintness, and simply praise.

Publications of Jay P. Dolan

Books

Transforming Parish Ministry: The Changing Roles of Catholic Clergy, Laity, and Women Religious in the United States, 1930–1980, Crossroad/Continuum Publishing Co., 1989, joint author with S. Appleby, P. Byrne, and D. Campbell; paperback edition, 1990.

The American Catholic Experience: A History from Colonial Times to the Present (New York, Doubleday & Company, Inc., 1985); paperback edition, 1987; French translation, Editions de Cerf, in process.

Catholic Revivalism: The American Experience 1830–1900 (University of Notre Dame Press, 1978); paperback edition, 1978.

The Immigrant Church: New York's Irish and German Catholics, 1815–1865 (Johns Hopkins University Press, 1975); paperback edition, 1977; received John Gilmary Shea Award, 1975, from American Catholic Historical Association.

Edited Books

Jay P. Dolan and Gilberto M. Hinojosa, eds. *Mexican Americans and the Catholic Church. 1900–1965,* University of Notre Dame Press, 1994, 352 pp.

Jay P. Dolan and Jaime R. Vidal, eds. *Puerto Rican and Cuban Catholics in the U.S. 1900–1965,* University of Notre Dame Press, 1994, 256 pp.

Jay P. Dolan and Allan Figueroa Deck, S.J., eds., *Hispanic Catholic Culture in the U.S.: Issues and Concerns,* University of Notre Dame Press, 1994, 480 pp.

New Dimensions in American Religious History, (eds., J. Dolan and James Wind) (Wm. B. Eerdmans Publishing Co., 1993), 329 pp.

The American Catholic Parish: A History from 1850 to the Present, 2 vols. (Paulist Press, 1987).

Heritage of '76, (ed.) (University of Notre Dame Press, 1976).

Edited Collection

American Catholic Tradition, 50 volumes (New York: Arno Press, 1978); served as advisory editor and wrote introductory essay for collection.

Articles

"The Search for an American Catholicism, 1780–1820," in *Religious Diversity and American Religious History,* ed. Walter H. Conser, Jr. and Sumner B. Twiss, University of Georgia Press, 1997, pp. 26–51.

"Catholicism and American Culture: Strategies for Survival," in *Minority Faiths and the American Protestant Mainstream,* ed. Jonathan D. Sarna, University of Illinois Press, 1997, pp. 61–80.

"The Search for an American Catholicism," *The Catholic Historical Review,* vol. 82, no. 2 (April 1996), pp. 169–186

"Patterns of Leadership in the Congregation," in James P. Wind and James W. Lewis (eds.), *American Congregations, vol. 2: New Perspectives in the Study of Congregations* (Chicago: University of Chicago Press, 1994), pp. 225–256.

"Conclusion," in Jay P. Dolan and Allan Figueroa Deck, S.J. (eds.) *Hispanic Catholic Culture in the U.S.* (University of Notre Dame Press, 1994), pp. 440–455.

"The People As Well As The Prelates: A Social History of a Denomination," in R. Mullin and R. Richey (eds.) *Reimagining Denominationalism: Interpretive Essays* (New York: Oxford University Press, 1994), pp. 43–57.

"New Directions in American Catholic History," (eds.) Jay P. Dolan and James P. Wind, *New Dimensions in American Religious History,* (Grand Rapids, MI: Wm. B. Eerdmans Publishing Co., 1993), pp. 152–174.

"The Desire for Democracy in the American Church," *A Democratic Catholic Church: The Reconstruction of Roman Catholicism,* eds. Eugene C. Bianchi and Rosemary Radford Ruether (New York: Crossroads, 1992), pp. 113–127.

"The Church of New York: Past and Present," *Thought,* Vol. 66, No. 263, 1991, pp. 376–386.

"From Coersion to Persuasion: The Rise of Religious Freedom," *All Imaginable Liberty: The Religious Liberty Clause of the First Amendment,* ed. Francis Graham Lee (Philadelphia, PA: St. Joseph University Press, 1990), pp. 17–32.

"Religion and the Immigrant Community: 1820–1920," *American Catholics,* ed. Joseph F. Kelly (Wilmington, DE: Michael Glazier, Inc., 1989), pp. 27–50.

"Being Catholic," *New Theology Review,* Vol. 2, No. 3, 1989, pp. 20–24.

"Religion and Social Change in the American Catholic Community," *Altered Landscapes: Christianity in America 1935–1985,* ed. David W. Lotz (Grand Rapids, MI: Wm. B. Eerdmans Publishing Co., 1989), pp. 42–60.

"Pastoral Practice of U.S. Priesthood-An Historical Perspective," *Resource for Continuing Formation of Clergy,* Vol. 16, pp. 21–28, 1988.

"The Immigrants and Their Gods: A New Perspective in American Religious History," *Church History,* Vol. 57, no. 1, March 1988, pp. 61–72.

"Immigration in American Christianity: A History of Their Histories," in *A Century of Church History: The Legacy of Philip Schaff,* ed. H. W. Bowden (Carbondale, Ill.: Southern Illinois Univ. Press, 1988), pp. 119–147.

"Catholic Attitudes Toward Protestants," in *Uncivil Religion: Interreligious Hostility in America,* ed., Robert N. Bellah and Frederick E. Greenspahn, (New York: Crossroad, 1987), pp. 72–86.

"The Parish in the American Past," in Mark Searle (ed.), *Parish: A Place For Worship,* Collegeville, Minnesota, Liturgical Press, 1981), pp. 25–39.

"Catholic Romance with Modernity," *The Wilson Quarterly,* 5 (Autumn 1981), pp. 120–33.

"American Catholicism and Modernity," *Cross Currents,* 21 (2) (Summer 1981), pp. 150–62.

"New Horizons in American Catholic Studies," in David Alvarez (ed.) *An American Church,* (Moraga, CA, 1979), pp. 1–7.

"Philadelphia and the German Catholic Community," in Randall M. Miller and Thomas O. Marzik (eds.) *Immigrants and Religion in Urban America,* (Temple University Press, 1977), pp. 69–83.

"American Catholics and Revival Religion, 1850–1900," *Horizons,* Journal of the College Theology Society, 3 (Spring 1976), pp. 39–57.

"Catholic Ethnics: Past and Present," *Liberty and Justice for All: Ethnicity and Race,* (Washington, DC: National Conference of Catholic Bishops, 1975), pp. 25–29.

"A Critical Period in American Catholicism," *Review of Politics,* 25 (October 1973), pp. 523–536.

"Immigrants in the City: New York's Irish and German Catholics," *Church History,* 41 (September, 1972), pp. 354–368.